Praise for *Masking and Unmasking Ourselves: Interpreting Biblical Texts on Clothing and Identity*

"Though nothing is likely to equal for me the power of Norman Cohen's classic *Self, Struggle and Change*, his most recent work, *Masking and Unmasking Ourselves*, is his most elegant and engrossing book to date. Though episodic in structure, this book unrolls like a single great story, and the deft interspersing of self-reflection—the consistent invitation to readers to try on the garment of his narrative for its fit to their own lives—is, as ever, gentle and engaging. In a style measured for the general reader, Rabbi Cohen speaks also to those familiar with the dress codes of midrash. We are in the hands of a master."

—**Peter Pitzele**, author, *Our Fathers' Wells: A Personal Encounter with the Myths of Genesis*

"From the simple fig leaf to Joseph's many colored coat to elaborate priestly and royal vestments, Norman Cohen pulls threads from Jewish tradition and deftly weaves them together into a wardrobe of surprising insight and wisdom."

—**Rabbi Sandy Eisenberg Sasso**, author, *God's Echo: Exploring Scripture with Midrash* and many books for children including *God's Paintbrush* and *In God's Name*

"Through the garment of midrash, Rabbi Cohen unfolds the intricate layers of Torah. In exploring clothing as a symbol, he invites readers to discover their own inner depths."

—**(Sr.) Mary C. Boys**, Skinner and McAlpin Professor of Practical Theology, Union Theological Seminary, New York City; coauthor, *Christians & Jews in Dialogue: Learning in the Presence of the Other*

"Norman Cohen's brilliantly informative assessment of clothing in Jewish texts and tradition suggests that we are what we wear. This wonderfully searching book holds up a mirror and prompts us to reflect on whether the world sees us as we see ourselves."

—**Peter J. Rubinstein**, senior rabbi, Central Synagogue, New York City

"From hero to harlot, from veil to vest, Cohen uncovers a deep layer of meaning and symbolism in the Torah when he explores the role of clothing, society and status in this fascinating and thoughtful book."
—**Rabbi Elyse Goldstein**, editor, *New Jewish Feminism, The Women's Torah Commentary, The Women's Haftarah Commentary;* author, *ReVisions: Seeing Torah from a Feminist Lens*

"From Scripture to Shakespeare, Cohen weaves an extended creative midrash ... covering and uncovering layers of meaning in ancient texts."
—**Rabbi Judith Abrams**, author, *The Other Talmud— The* Yerushalmi: *Unlocking the Secrets of* The Talmud of Israel *for Judaism Today*

"In this compassionate meditation on the human condition—wearing the garb of ten studies of biblical clothing—our teacher Rabbi Norman Cohen again demonstrates that Torah is the appropriate dressing to cure the ailment of Adam's mortality."
—**Rabbi Burton L. Visotzky**, Appleman Professor of Midrash and Interreligious Studies, The Jewish Theological Seminary; author, *Sage Tales: Wisdom and Wonder from the Rabbis of the Talmud*

"Long have we waited for an illuminating study of the biblical mystique of clothes. Thanks now to the lively and thoughtful prose of Cohen, we wait no more."
—**Phyllis Tribble**, Baldwin Professor of Sacred Literature, Emerita, Union Theological Seminary

"Norman Cohen is one of the great midrashists of our generation. He offers us a 'wardrobe' of depth meditations on clothing in the Hebrew Bible and therefore, also, on candor and deception in our own lives. With eye-popping surprises on almost every page, Cohen invites us to reconsider our own disguises (and any visit to the tailor)!"
—**Lawrence Kushner**, Emanu-El Scholar, Congregation Emanu-El of San Francisco; author, *Kabbalah: A Love Story; I'm God; You're Not: Observations on Organized Religion and Other Disguises of the Ego;* and *God Was in This Place and I, i Did Not Know: Finding Self, Spirituality and Ultimate Meaning*

MASKING
AND
*Un*MASKING
OURSELVES

Other Jewish Lights Books by Norman J. Cohen

Hineini in Our Lives:
Learning How to Respond to Others through
14 Biblical Texts & Personal Stories

Moses and the Journey to Leadership:
Timeless Lessons of Effective Management from
the Bible and Today's Leaders

Self, Struggle & Change:
Family Conflict Stories in Genesis and
Their Healing Insights for Our Lives

Voices from Genesis:
Guiding Us through the Stages of Life

The Way Into Torah

MASKING
AND
*Un*MASKING
OURSELVES

Interpreting Biblical Texts on
Clothing & Identity

DR. NORMAN J. COHEN

For People of All Faiths, All Backgrounds
JEWISH LIGHTS Publishing
Woodstock, Vermont

Walking Together, Finding the Way®
SKYLIGHT PATHS®
PUBLISHING
Woodstock, Vermont

Masking and Unmasking Ourselves:
Interpreting Biblical Texts on Clothing & Identity

2012 Hardcover Edition, First Printing
© 2012 by Norman J. Cohen

Library of Congress Cataloging-in-Publication Data
Cohen, Norman J.
Masking and unmasking ourselves : interpreting biblical texts on clothing & identity / Norman J. Cohen.
p. cm.
Includes bibliographical references.
ISBN 978-1-58023-461-0
1. Biblical costume. 2. Biblical costume—Symbolic aspects. 3. Clothing and dress—Religious aspects—Judaism. 4. Bible. O.T.—Criticism, interpretation, etc. I. Title.
BS680.C65C64 2012
221.8'391—dc23
2011051295

10 9 8 7 6 5 4 3 2 1

Manufactured in the United States of America
Jacket design: Jenny Buono
Interior design: Tim Holtz

Published by Jewish Lights Publishing and SkyLight Paths Publishing
Divisions of Longhill Partners, Inc.
Sunset Farm Offices, Route 4, P.O. Box 237
Woodstock, VT 05091
Tel: (802) 457-4000   Fax: (802) 457-4004
www.jewishlights.com   www.skylightpaths.com

To my students at
Hebrew Union College–Jewish Institute of Religion,
who over the years have enabled me to share my passion for
Torah study while giving me their gifts of insight, interest,
commitment, and hope for the future.

Contents

Preface

An emperor who cares for nothing but his wardrobe hires two weavers who promise him the finest suit of clothes made from a fabric invisible to anyone who is unfit for his position or just hopelessly stupid. The emperor cannot see the cloth himself but pretends that he can for fear of appearing unsuitable for his role; his ministers do the same. When the swindlers report that the suit is finished, they dress him in mime, and the emperor then marches in procession before his subjects. A child in the crowd calls out that the emperor is wearing nothing at all, and the cry is taken up by others. The emperor cringes, suspecting the assertion is true, but holds himself up proudly and continues the procession.[1]

Hans Christian Andersen's famous Danish children's tale was published in 1837. His manuscript was at the printers when he decided to change the original climax of the tale from the emperor's subjects admiring the invisible clothes to that of the child's cry. Most scholars feel that the change was motivated by Andersen's desire to expose the hypocrisy and snobbery of the Danish bourgeoisie.[2]

The symbolic power of clothing, both in terms of what it hides as well as what it reveals, has everything to do with identity and how we perceive it. In Andersen's tale, the invisible suit of clothing tells us as readers much about the character of the emperor as well as that of his subjects. As a literary symbol, it also reveals the writer's concerns and values and those of the society in which the writer lives. The emperor's clothing emphasizes that our task as readers is not only to decipher what a particular garment symbolizes but also to pare away layers of clothing in order to gain a sense of what lies underneath. It is always more than what appears on the surface.

So it was with the medieval Jewish mystics, the kabbalists. Moses de Leon, the author of the key thirteenth-century mystical text the *Zohar*, describes the Torah as a bride covered with layers of garments that conceal her innermost beauty. In this mystical imaging, biblical narratives are merely the outermost garments that are visible to all readers. Listen to the words of the *Zohar*:

> Whoever thinks that the [outer] garment is the real Torah ... will have no share in the world that is coming. That is why David said: "Open my eyes, so I can perceive the wonders of Your teaching" (Psalm 119:18), what is under the garment of Torah![3]
>
> Come and see: There is a garment visible to all. When ... fools see someone in a good-looking garment, they look no further. But the essence of the garment is the body; the essence of the body is the soul!
>
> So it is with Torah.... This body is clothed in garments: stories of this world.
>
> Fools of the world look only at that garment, the story of Torah; they know nothing more. They do not look at what is under that garment. Those who know more do not look at the garment, but rather at the body under the garment....
>
> As wine must sit in a jar, so Torah must sit in this garment. So look only at what is under the garment. All those words, all those stories are [mere] garments.[4]

Although the Torah needs layers of outer garments if it is to be preserved in this world, divine truths are hidden within. The surface meaning of the text is seen as merely the first of several garmentlike layers concealing deeper meaning. As Michael Fishbane, the noted scholar of biblical and rabbinic literature, and currently professor of Jewish studies at the Divinity School of the University of Chicago, has so beautifully written about these kabbalistic notions, "The true hermeneut [interpreter] ... will be drawn to this garmented bride [the Torah] and will strip away the garments of Torah until he and the beloved are one."[5]

The kabbalists understood the Torah to be an inexhaustible well that contains many layers of potential meaning. These different levels of meaning are divided into four categories, designated by the word *PaRDeS*, an acronym for *peshat* (literal), *remez* (allegorical), *derash* (midrashic), and *sod* (mystical).[6] These are succeeding levels of depth that the reader can plumb.

Similarly, the Rabbis of old recognized that there are "seventy faces" to the Torah, only the first of which was the *peshat*.[7] The Bible, therefore, possesses multiple layers of meaning that are latent in every syntactical and lexical item, in every aspect of the narrative line. Interpretation need only uncover what is concealed in the text.[8]

To find the meanings inherent in the biblical text, the Rabbinic process of interpretation, midrash, initially involves focusing on what is presented in the Bible: every word, phrase, symbol, indeed every letter. However, only elements that are crucial are provided to the reader; all else is often obscure. Time and place are frequently undefined; the thoughts, feelings, and motivations of the characters remain submerged.[9] The reader then must move beyond the *peshat*, the surface meaning, and pay attention to these gaps in the text, the places where the Bible is silent. Midrash is the art of entering these interstices, exploring every possible meaning.[10] Rather than being obstacles for the reader to overcome, the general lack of details in the Bible and the lack of clarity in the use of language therefore present readers in every generation—us—with opportunities to find new meanings.

Let us then begin the process of trying to find meaning for our lives by finding our way into ever-deepening levels of the Torah text, uncovering layers of her garments as we strive to become one with the Bride.

Introduction

One could say that I am an avid fan of the New York Yankees. I know intellectually that baseball is only a game, but occasionally I seem to live and die with every pitch thrown. So you can just imagine the scene on the evening of November 4, 2001, as I sat watching the bottom of the ninth inning of the seventh and final game of the World Series. My Yankees were about to beat the Arizona Diamondbacks and win their fourth consecutive world championship. Of course they would win, since I was wearing every article of Yankees clothing that I possessed: Yankees cap, pinstripe shirt, socks, even underwear emblazoned with the intersecting NY logo. My Yankees attire had proved so many times to possess magical powers that a victory was guaranteed. And to boot, the incomparable pitcher, Mariano Rivera, who had struck out all three batters he faced in the eighth inning and had not lost a lead in twenty-three straight playoff games, was set to "close" the game and give us a 2–1 victory.

But my sports world collapsed when a shallow, looping single drove in the Diamondbacks's winning run. That one hit by Jose Gonzalez, affectionately known as "Gonzo," ended both the Yankee mystique and my surety that I as a fan had the power to affect the outcome of a game by controlling both natural and supernatural forces through the power of Yankees paraphernalia.

Such a belief in the magical powers of clothing and ornaments was not invented by the first baseball fan. Primitive human beings, beset by a plethora of fears in a frightening world of discovery,

1

sought to protect themselves by attributing animistic power to inanimate objects.[1]

Through their body paint, garments, and ornamental objects, they sought to control the forces that dominated their lives. Painting yellow ocher on their bodies enabled them to tap the power of the sun; bones and animal skins gave them the strength and stealth of animals that preyed upon them.[2]

This belief in the supernatural power of clothing and ornaments has been widespread throughout human history and persists even today. Magic rings and cloaks of invincibility have not disappeared; they simply no longer appear in their original forms and are not used in the service of magic on a conscious level. For example, ordinary objects with no inherent magical qualities are worn by many people inside out in order to reverse fortunes. What are "rally hats," which are seen in baseball parks when fans try to "cause" their team to come from behind and win, if not a subconscious amulet?[3] The definition of dress as it involves symbolic power includes not only garments but also hairstyles, makeup, body decorations, and jewelry.[4] These stylistic items also differentiate the qualities that the individual wearer possesses or wishes to possess. Sometimes, the person wearing these articles of fashion is not even consciously aware of the motivation. Fashion can tap deep-seated sources of emotion and need.[5]

Clothing is, indeed, a crucial element in every human context and reveals much about the individuals who wear it. As Polonius advises his son Leartes in *Hamlet*, "The apparel oft proclaims the man." He draws our attention to the integral relationship between what a person wears and who he or she is in Shakespeare's England.[6] Especially in the realm of literature, clothes assume a primary importance as a vehicle that suggests character, predicts a person's identity, and even governs it. Whether it is Madam Hester in Hawthorne's *Scarlet Letter* or Miss Havisham in Dickens's *Great Expectations*, clothes truly "make the person."[7]

But the problem is that if Oscar Wilde is correct that "if you give a man a mask, he will tell you the truth," then what exactly conveys the truth? Is it the person him or herself or is it the mask, the clothing that he or she wears, that reveals deeper images of the self? It has been noted, for example, that Clark Kent and Superman are actually one person, with the mild-mannered reporter being the "mask" for the superhuman alien (just as the kabbalists believed that when angels descend into this world they must appear as human beings if they are to endure). Yet, if Superman is Clark Kent, then Lois Lane and Clark actually love each other ... but they don't.[8] It is clear that the boundaries between self and not self are very ambiguous, and the clothing people wear at times obfuscates who the person really is. All we have to do is listen to ourselves the next time we are trying on new clothing and ask ourselves, "Is it really me?"[9]

Even though clothes sometimes create greater ambiguity in defining the person—that is, it is hard to know whether they are being worn as mere "costume" or whether they are important signs that tell us about the true self[10]—we have no choice but to take clothing as serious nonverbal communication. Clothing can provide important information about the sex, age, occupation, origin, personality, attitudes, and values of the wearer.[11]

Clothing can be crucial in terms of image construction and interpretation; it can give us insight into a person's sense of self as well as the picture of his or her ideal self.[12] For example, we see this very clearly in the culture of branding that defines contemporary politics. The press noted, for instance, that President Obama, in his first day on the job at the White House, was photographed in the Oval Office without a suit jacket and wearing rolled-up sleeves in order to portray a more informal culture and identification with the masses.[13]

Not to be outdone by her husband in this regard, First Lady Michelle Obama was recently seen shopping in a Target store in Alexandria, Virginia, wearing a baseball cap, very casual clothes, and sunglasses. The supposed disguise worked well when she was barely recognized, but her picture was transmitted around the world. Chided as being a fashionista and based on the White House's desire to portray both her and her husband as down-to-earth and "one of the people," this was a wonderful political Kodak moment. Though the White House stressed that it was not uncommon for the First Lady to slip out of the White House and run errands, an Associated Press White House photographer was tipped off and was there to get the shot.[14]

Consultants get paid huge salaries for making wardrobe decisions for politicians. It was reported that Al Gore hired a feminist consultant at a salary of $15,000 a month during the 2000 campaign to give him a "makeover" from an alpha to a beta male.[15]

Clothes are consciously used to define, present, and reveal, but also to conceal and deceive; to communicate, but also to intentionally miscommunicate in complex ways.[16] For example, modern writers have noted that clothes that simultaneously conceal and reveal—like a half-opened gift—invite us to imagine what lies beneath. Covering the body does not necessarily discourage sexual interest, but it is a device for arousing it.[17]

Buying and wearing clothing, therefore, are creative acts by which we humans participate in the formulation of our self-image. Even as we conceal our naked bodies, we may be revealing our inner core, our souls.[18]

Of all of the conscious and unconscious reasons for choosing clothing, the pursuit of status is a key driving force behind fashion.[19]

For thousands of years, clothes have indicated status and identified individuals as members of particular groups—who is in and who is out.[20]

The concern over who is wearing what and the relationship between dress and social status led to the enactment of Sumptuary Laws in Elizabethan England. Though ostensibly meant to prevent wasteful economic extravagance,[21] they served to proscribe or forbid the wearing of certain styles of clothes by specific classes of people.

Clothes can be signs of social status, position, and power,[22] and in most societies this also is very evident in the religious realm. Religious vestments, only worn by recognized religious authorities, originally were thought to possess magical, holy powers. Priests of every religion were identified by their dress. Though today it generally is merely symbolic, liturgical dress still identifies group affiliation.[23]

Clothes are indeed badges of identity, and our choice of clothes is a powerful indicator of the group to which we belong. For example, Gandhi and other Indian nationalists asked Indians to strip off their European clothing and cast them into "sacrificial bonfires," encouraging them to wear *khadi*, spun and handwoven cloth.[24] There are many who felt that Gandhi's loincloth transcended the limitations of language itself to express his most important messages regarding Indian identity.[25]

However, we often choose to belong to different groups, and the clothes we put on for one group can clash with another. These conflicts can involve different cultural and social values and norms.[26] As individuals attempt to bridge different worlds, they constantly are "dressing and undressing," assuming and then casting aside these identities. Notwithstanding Gandhi's influence, working under the British rule, most Indians typically would indeed wear British sartorial splendor but would change back into Indian garb *before* entering their homes. The threshold of the house was a point of transformation.[27]

Whatever the contexts in which clothes are worn, they are often the most powerful forms of communication. As in any great literature, the language of putting on and taking off clothing in the Bible, and especially the narratives that turn on the symbolic use of clothes, can provide us as readers with a sense of the overarching worldview of the biblical writers. Yet, by immersing ourselves in the symbolic language and stories of the Bible, we can also gain much insight into ourselves and our own lives.

As we embark on our journey of engaging ten paradigmatic biblical stories that involve clothing in an essential way, it is not simply a matter of learning about the biblical text, about the characters and their interactions, but rather involves confronting our own life dramas, our own stories. Torah is a mirror: when we gaze into it, it reflects back to us our own personalities, ambivalences, struggles, and potential for growth. As we uncover the "garments of Torah," we will come to reveal that which may heretofore be concealed by our own layers of insulation.

1

DIVINE GARMENTS OF CREATION

Concealing Our Nakedness, Revealing Our Inner Core

Genesis 3:7–21

" … Ye cedars with innumerable boughs
Hide me, where I may never see them more.
But let us now, as in bad plight, devise
What best may for the present serve to hide
The parts of each from other that seem most
To shame obnoxious, and unseemliest seen.
Some tree whose broad smooth leaves together sewed,
And girded on our loins, may cover round
Those middle parts, that this newcomer, Shame,
There sit not, and reproach us as unclean."
So counseled he, and both went
Into the thickest wood; there soon they chose
The fig-tree, not that kind for fruit renowned….
And with what skill they had, together sewed,
To gird their waist, vain covering if to hide
Their guilt and dreaded shame, O how unlike
To that first naked glory!

> John Milton
> *Paradise Lost*, 1667

7

A Miraculous Garment of Light

According to the Rabbinic tradition, Adam was not the first to clothe himself with garments. God is pictured as being covered with divine light (in Hebrew, *'or*) in order to create the world.[1] Even though the Bible begins with God creating the heavens and earth, which is followed by the creation of light at the beginning of Genesis, the Rabbis emphasized that only after God illuminated the world with a garment of light, perhaps the luster of God's majesty, did the Divine actually begin to create.[2] In effect, the act of Creation was God covering the entire world with a tentlike garment of light,[3] and all the world, including the first human beings, were the products of that divine light. Adam and Eve possessed that light, which surely symbolized their godlike potential.

In fact, God is portrayed in the tradition as wearing seven different garments that would be worn successively from the creation of the world to the messianic era. These include garments of majesty, strength, vengeance, zeal, righteousness, compassion, and purity.[4] Many individual verses in the Bible describe God as "wearing" these and other qualities.[5] Then, in the end of days, God is pictured as a bridegroom adorned with a royal diadem, Israel is described as a bride bedecked in her finery, and the Messiah will be covered with the very same primordial garment of light whose splendor radiates from one end of the world to the other (Isaiah 61:10).[6]

The garments worn by the Divine clearly represent the key attributes that enabled all the major events of Jewish history to take place, including the crossing of the Red Sea, the giving of the Torah on Mount Sinai, and Israel's battles for survival against the nations of the world.[7] Because clothes and ornaments define identity, each of us as readers is forced to identify the "garments" we wear, those that we possess or hope to possess. All of us must confront who we are, even as we measure ourselves against the ideal fabric of the Divine. Can we even recognize our own garments, our own qualities? And then, by virtue of how we live, are we able to don those garments that will enable us to experience the light of God's Presence that can bring us to wholeness, return us to the pristine experience of the Creation and the Garden?

In the beginning, Adam and Eve were indeed covered by garments of divine light, befitting their initial purity and perfection.[8] However, because they were totally covered by the light, they were not at all aware of their underlying nakedness and, as such, felt no attendant shame (Genesis 2:25).[9]

Confronting Our Nakedness and Shame

Yet, the instant that Adam and Eve transgressed God's sole commandment not to eat the fruit of the Tree of Knowledge, the protective covering disappeared, and immediately they became aware of their nakedness.[10] Their eyes were opened, and they realized that they had suffered a great loss—the garment of light that God shared with them and the wholeness that it brought. They lost their oneness with the Divine and, in the process, their own sense of unity as well. They were forced to recognize their essential differences and had to relate to each other in a wholly different manner. This caused each of them to feel embarrassed and ashamed (Genesis 3:7).

A modern example of nakedness engendering vulnerability and embarrassment involves President Lyndon Johnson. Richard Goodwin, a former speech writer and aide to LBJ, experienced the typical Johnson outrages, which included a meeting the president held with his closest policy advisors that took place in the heated pool in the White House. Amazingly, Johnson insisted that all of the participants be in the nude.[11]

In writing his recollections of Johnson in his memoir about the 1960s, which in the main are based on the diaries he kept from 1964 to 1967, Goodwin documented such outrageous behavior. It was clear to Goodwin that it demonstrated Johnson's paranoia. For example, he was afraid that meetings were being taped and details leaked. As a result, Johnson attempted to exert his authority and power, thus making his advisors feel totally vulnerable. The naked meeting in the pool had that effect on his staff.

Goodwin writes:

> Suspended motionless in the water ... I felt Johnson's immense vitality—intense, forceful and direct.... I felt uncomfortable, almost dimensionless, could not feel, sense my body, the slow sustaining movement of my arms. There was only the powerful flow of Johnson's will.[12]

When human beings are naked in front of others, bereft of garments that cover and enhance their image, they are deprived of their humanity.

Such depravation occurred during the Holocaust when the Nazis forced Jews to strip naked in many different public contexts, but especially in the concentration camps. Surely, one of the purposes was to utilize their clothing and possessions for a variety of purposes. More than that, their heads also were shaved, and the Germans used the hair for pillows and mattresses. Whatever ulterior motives they had, the Nazis also succeeded in dehumanizing the Jews. Forcing them to be naked, they demonstrated that Jews were less than human.

In the Bible, nakedness is also symbolic of sinfulness, and myriad prophetic texts utilize the image of the stripping of garments as a way of revealing a person's sinful acts. In fact, one of the most oft-used phrases by the prophets (or a version of it) is the "uncovering of one's nakedness," which underscores this symbolism. Note, for example, the typical wording in Ezekiel:

> Thus said the Lord God: Because of your brazen effrontery, offering your nakedness to your lovers for harlotry ... I will expose your nakedness and all shall [see it].... They shall strip you of your clothing and take away your dazzling jewelry, leaving you naked and bare.
>
> (Ezekiel 16:36–39)[13]

Uncovering people's nakedness also reveals their shame. The prophet Isaiah poetically captures the power of the symbolic removal of the garments of sinners, in this case, the daughters of Zion:

> In that day, Adonai will strip off the finery of the anklets, the fillets, and the crescents; ... the bracelets and the veils; the turbans, the armlets and the sashes; ... the festive robes, the mantles and the shawls; ... the lace gowns and the linen vests; and the kerchiefs and the capes.
>
> *And then—*
> *Instead of perfume, there shall be rot;*
> *And instead of an apron, a rope;*
> *Instead of a diadem of beaten-work,*
> *A shorn head; Instead of a rich robe,*
> *A girding of sackcloth; A burn instead of beauty.*
>
> (Isaiah 3:18–24)

Without the use of a single verb in the final verse, and with the stark repetition of the word "instead," we feel the deprivation, loss, humiliation, barrenness, and shame of the once proud, wealthy, and bedecked sinner.[14]

Though far removed from the Garden of Eden, we understand that occasionally our actions uncover our core natures, thereby impelling us to see ourselves for what we truly are. We, like Adam and Eve, reveal our own imperfections, and if we are honest with ourselves, this can be truly devastating. It is ultimately impossible for us to camouflage our self-knowledge, the stark truth of who we are, and we are left with the question of how can we overcome our resultant feelings of vulnerability and shame.

What Lies under the Fig Leaves?

The Bible has several examples in which individuals who feel vulnerable in the face of others cover themselves as a means of protection. When Rebecca first laid eyes upon Isaac, she was overcome by him; feelings of astonishment, awe, and vulnerability overwhelmed her, and she fell off the camel upon which she was riding (Genesis 24:64). It is almost as if she could not bear to look at him, and she immediately took her veil and covered herself. She instinctively knew that she needed to protect herself in his presence.[15]

Perhaps the most powerful instance of covering oneself in order to overcome vulnerability occurred when Moses came down from Mount Sinai bearing the two tablets. He was not aware that his face was radiant with the light of the Divine, but the people, seeing his face, shrank before him. As a result, Moses donned a veil to protect the people and enable him to speak to them without them being afraid (Exodus 34:29–35). He himself was covered with divine light (*'or*) but needed to wear a veil to help the people of Israel overcome the shame and vulnerability they felt.[16] The Rabbis also suggest that before Israel sinned by building the Golden Calf, they indeed were able to witness the divine light of Sinai without being afraid as they stood at the foot of the mountain. Yet, following their sin, they could not even look upon the face of Moses, their intermediary before the Divine.[17]

In reflecting on this incident, perhaps we should consider those moments in which we have felt the most vulnerable as we faced the "other" in our lives, be that other God or the individuals whom we love and with whom we interact. Dare we ask what we might have done on those occasions that made us feel vulnerable and ashamed, to the point of not being able to look that person in the face?

Having eaten from the tree, Adam and Eve's eyes were opened; they became aware of their nakedness and, as a result, the stark differences between the two of them. They, too, felt vulnerable and ashamed. Their oneness had been broken, and as they stood facing each other for the very first time, they were astonished by how their bodies were shaped. Recognizing their maleness and femaleness, they also instinctively had to cover themselves, cover their shame.[18]

They sewed together fig leaves, making loincloths (in Hebrew, *chagorot*, from the verb meaning "to gird") for themselves (Genesis 3:7). They literally "girded" their loins as a means of protecting themselves. Their actions prompt each of us to further reflect upon the "garments" we instinctively use to protect and perhaps insulate ourselves as we become aware of our own shameful actions. How do we camouflage our guilt so we do not have to witness it? How do we rationalize what we've done to assuage our own conscience?

But we as readers also must ponder why Adam and Eve chose to cover themselves with fig leaves when they had all the trees in the Garden at their disposal. The Rabbis suggest that the very object that led them astray now became the vehicle that would protect them.[19] According to the thrust of the Rabbinic tradition, the tree from which they ate in the Garden and that had led to their punishment and pain was none other than a fig tree.[20]

Amazingly then, Adam and Eve wore the very symbol of their sinful act, ever reminding them of what they did, just as we all carry with us the memories of past deeds that we regret and that continue to haunt us. But perhaps there is more here, because the vehicle of their downfall is transformed into an object that can protect them. Is it possible for us to repair ourselves by recognizing and owning past acts and, in so doing, underscore our desire to embrace our higher selves? In what way do we carry with us the remnants of past actions, which are both constant reminders of how we have fallen short and also goads for change? For the first human beings, the fig leaves represented a reminder of their base sides, but also of their potential for change and uplift.

Hide and Go Seek among the Trees of the Garden

However, the fig leaves turned out to be a flimsy camouflage not at all suitable to hide Adam and Eve's nakedness and their sin.[21] The garments that they produced could not cover their entire bodies, and they were left exposed. As a result, these first human beings sought to hide among the trees of the Garden (Genesis 3:8), attempting in a sense to cover themselves more extensively. Adam and Eve hoped that the trees of the Garden would hide their sin.

Some midrashim extend the theme that the tree from which they ate was the very tree they used to cover themselves—the fig tree—by adding that it also was the tree under which Adam and Eve attempted to hide.[22] Even though they had covered themselves, they could not hide from the Divine. The creations could never hide from the Creator, as Elie Wiesel, Holocaust survivor and chronicler, Nobel laureate, and prolific Jewish writer, paraphrased God's admonishment of them: "Tell me, you who are hiding, do you really believe that the house can hide from its builder?"[23]

Adam and Eve experienced the Divine Presence, which according to some midrashim only appeared to them once they took the initiative of covering themselves, indicating that they acknowledged what they had done.[24] Nevertheless, Adam admitted, "I heard the sound of You in the Garden, and I was afraid because I was still naked, and I hid" (Genesis 3:10). Mere fig leaves could not camouflage their essential flawed natures. The Rabbis emphasize that God had given Adam and Eve only one commandment, which they failed to observe, and now they were naked, bare, and hiding from both God and their deed that caused them shame.[25] The protective garment that had covered them, the light of the Divine, which symbolizes the Torah in the Rabbinic tradition, disappeared. Because clothing or the lack thereof is indicative of our inner character, our human qualities, which is underscored by the fact that both are described as "habit,"[26] Adam himself is pictured as understanding the nature of his actions. He said, "In that very hour, my eyes were opened, and forthwith I knew that I was bare of the righteousness with which I had been clothed, and I wept and said to [God]: 'Why hast Thou done this to me in that You have deprived me of my glory with which I was clothed?'"[27]

But the Divine had compassion for the first man and woman. God could not banish them from paradise, sending them into the harsh world outside the Garden without some degree of protection. Like a good parent, God could not desert them, abandon them. The Divine wanted to shield them from the elements they would encounter.[28]

The Divine Tailor

So God made garments of skin (in Hebrew, *katnot 'or*) to clothe Adam and Eve following their transgression and prior to their expulsion (Genesis 3:21). The Rabbis generally accept the straightforward, simple meaning of this verse, that the garments were made of animal skins.[29] However, the obvious difference in the description of the fig leaves sewn by Adam and Eve—*chagorot*, which means some type of girdle or loincloth—and the garments made by God—*kutanot*, from the Hebrew word *kutonet*, which clearly means a full garment, like a coat—led the Rabbis to more creative possibilities.

The most poignant suggestion is that the garments were made of the skin shed by the serpent in the Garden.[30] Just imagine! The very vehicle of their sin and banishment from Eden was used by God to make the garments that would protect the first human beings outside of paradise, in the world of imperfection. On the one hand, they carried with them from the Garden of Eden a constant reminder of their sinfulness and demise; they would ever be enveloped by the serpent. Yet, the very objects from which they couldn't escape also served as their protection and the vehicle for their survival.

A few midrashim even stress that God intentionally covered Adam and Eve with "garments of honor."[31] Some suggest that the clothes were made of very bright, colorful animal skins, either the skins of a *tachash*, perhaps a dolphin, which were used later in the building of the Tabernacle,[32] or those of the Leviathan, the sea creature that is part of messianic mythology, whose skin is said to have had a luster to it.[33] Others identify the coverings with the priestly garments worn subsequently in the Temple, because the identical Hebrew expression, *yalbisheim kutanot* ("dressed them in garments"), is used in Leviticus 8:13 as well as in other biblical verses describing the priestly vestments. These interpretations indicate that the Rabbis believed that God would forgive Adam and Eve's sin.[34]

If clothing is indicative of inner character, how can we, ourselves, transform the reminders and memories of our failures and egregious actions into "garments" that can adorn and sustain us? Do we even believe it is possible for us as flawed human beings to change in this manner, or are leopard spots permanent?

The Reappearance of the Garments of Light

God's embrace of Adam and Eve is underscored even more in the tradition by a frequent interpretation of the "garments of skin ['or]" as "garments of light ['or]." The words for "skin" and "light" in Hebrew are homonyms, and there was even a belief that a Torah manuscript existed that described the garments that God made as actual "garments of light."[35] This play on words allows us as readers to extend the notion of our power as human beings to transform the skin of the snake into symbols of our repentance and thereby to return to God. Once again, Adam and Eve—and, by extension, every reader in every generation—can don the primordial light, the symbol of wholeness.[36] The garments of skin can become the original garment of light with which God enveloped the entire world.

The garments were thought to possess not only extraordinary brilliance and splendor but also exceptional power.[37] As such, the Rabbis said that these garments were among the ten things created in the twilight of the sixth day of Creation, prior to the onset of the first Sabbath.[38] Before God banished Adam and Eve from Eden following their sin, God provided them with the vehicles that would enable them to survive in the world outside the Garden and ensure that someday they would return to paradise.

But just picture the beginning of their sojourn outside of their Garden paradise, the moment at the end of that first Sabbath as the sun was setting. Adam became terrified, thinking that the darkness, or perhaps the serpent, would come and attack (perhaps envelop) them.[39] What did God do? Some midrashim suggest that God gave them a pillar of light to guard them from all the evil they would encounter,[40] while others say that God provided Adam with two flints, which he struck together, causing light to come forth.[41] In both cases, Adam then extended his hands toward the light and uttered a blessing, recalling the verse in Psalms, "[In] the night, the light was about me," that is, "covered" or "protected me" (Psalm 139:11). The tradition suggests that this is the origin of the blessing over the flame—light, fire—that is part of the *Havdalah* ritual at the end of the Sabbath, separating the holiness of the Sabbath from the rest of the days of the week: "Praised are you, Adonai, Ruler of the universe, who creates the flames of fire."[42]

In the *Havdalah* ceremony, when this blessing is recited over the flame using a braided candle, individuals extend their hands toward the flame and gaze at their fingers, which are bent toward them, thereby demonstrating the difference between light and darkness. Yet, the tradition also suggests that they should focus on their fingertips, as the fingernails reflect the light and appear much whiter.[43] This custom, which gained popularity among the medieval mystics, the kabbalists, can be understood as a reminder that in the Garden of Eden, Adam and Eve were originally covered by God with a protective skin (*'or*) and that all that is left of this protective garment, in a sense, the divine light (*'or*) of Eden, is what we carry with us on the tips of our fingers.

And each week, at the conclusion of the Sabbath, which is known in the Rabbinic tradition as "a day of all light," we, the progeny of Adam and Eve, gazing at our fingertips, look back nostalgically to both the perfection of the Sabbath as well as the original light of Creation and the Garden. At the same time, we look forward to one day returning to Eden and experiencing the wholeness and perfection that we taste each week on the Sabbath.

Carrying God's Garments with Us

The first human beings did not leave the Garden empty-handed. They left the Garden of their infancy covered by the garments that God had made for them. Adam and Eve carried a part of Eden with them. In time, Adam bequeathed the garments to his son Seth, who in turn gave them to Methusaleh, and he transmitted them to Noah, who took them on the ark in order to preserve them for the time when the world would be re-created following the Flood. Noah's firstborn son, Ham, then carried them off the ark, and they eventually passed to Nimrod and to subsequent generations.[44]

So we must ask whether we have been able to transmit garments that are symbolic of the best and highest that every human being possesses to our own progeny, to those who come after us. What are the garments that we have handed down to our children? What values and qualities do they represent? And do they wear those garments, or are they relegated to a dark corner of their closets, never to see the light of day?

Because according to the Rabbinic tradition the light was synonymous with Torah, the mystics believed that the good deeds of human beings, their observance of God's commandments, were sewn into radiant garments that would adorn the righteous in every generation and eventually would be worn by them as they enter the World to Come.[45]

2
NOAH'S GARMENTS AFTER THE FLOOD

Ensuring Protection or Covering Shame?

Genesis 9:20–24

The garments that God had made for Adam and Eve prior to their banishment from the Garden of Eden were handed down through the generations and now were in the possession of Noah and his sons.

Noah lived ten generations after Adam and Eve, but he still wore the garments of Eden.

Noah's appearance coincides with the onset of the Flood, when God returned the world to the void that existed prior to Creation, to a time when only water covered the earth. As God caused the waters to subside on the third day of Creation, gathering them together to allow dry land to appear and vegetation to grow (Genesis 1:9), so the floodwaters of Noah's day withdrew after forty days and nights. When Adam and Eve were created on the sixth day, they entered a world that could sustain them, and God blessed them, saying, "Be fruitful and multiply, and fill the earth" (Genesis 1:28). Noah and his family exited from the womblike ark that protected them, just as Adam and Eve had to leave the Garden that enveloped them, and Noah received the very same blessing (Genesis 9:1). However, Noah found a world totally destroyed and barren.

Noah: The Tiller of the Soil

Unlike the six days of Creation, in which God caused the earth to give forth vegetation to sustain humankind and then planted a Garden in Eden (Genesis 2:8–9), following the Deluge Noah had to till the soil himself. While Adam and Eve were placed like children in the Garden that protected them, a setting already lush with every type of tree that was pleasing to the sight and good for food, this "second creation" would depend on the work of Noah's own hands. He, himself, would have to re-create God's Garden.

Noah would have to work the earth and plant all sorts of fruits and vegetables in order to sustain himself and his family (Genesis 9:20).[1] The curious detail noted in the Bible that he specifically planted a vineyard following the Flood that destroyed the world clearly has its origins in a universal folkloristic motif. Deucalion, for example, the hero of the Deluge in the Greek myth of Dionysus, who introduced wine making, is just one parallel to the story of Noah and the Flood.[2]

According to some interpretations, when Noah left the ark, as he began to clear and plow the ground, he found a vine twig with roots that had come from the Garden of Eden.[3] Others say that in preparation for the Flood, Noah loaded all the possible plants for future cultivation onto the ark, including the vine shoot to plant a vineyard.[4] Not only has it been suggested by the Rabbis that this vine shoot had been taken out of the Garden by Adam when he was banished, but most powerfully, that the Tree of Knowledge from which Adam ate was indeed a grapevine! The forbidden fruit, therefore, was the wine that Adam consumed, for, according to the tradition, there is nothing that brings suffering to humankind more than wine.[5]

Read in this light, Adam carried the protective garments of light with him from Eden and also the object of his sin. However, the tradition emphasizes that Noah, who was in essence the re-created Adam following the Flood, should have learned from the mistakes of his antediluvian ancestor. Following Noah's planting of the vineyard and becoming drunk from the wine he produced (Genesis 9:20–21), God is pictured as castigating Noah, "What are you doing in this vineyard? Was not Adam punished with mortality just because of the wine?"[6]

However, Noah learned nothing from Adam. "Noah, the man of the earth, began [va-yachel] by planting [of all things] a vineyard" (Genesis 9:20). A similar Hebrew root (ch-l-l) means "to profane," underscoring that Noah acted sinfully, thus profaning himself. As a result, he no longer was called a "wholly righteous man" (Genesis 6:9) but rather is described as "a man of the earth." The earth (in Hebrew, adamah) was cursed due to Adam's sin in the Garden (Genesis 3:17), and now Noah was to be identified both with the accursed earth and with Adam, whose very name is associated with the earth, and with his sin. Adam and Noah were seen in this regard as "earthy men"—ignorant and sinful.[7]

Noah was the heir to Eden, carrying with him the divine garments, which protected him as they did Adam and symbolized God's embrace and Noah's potential for wholeness. He also possessed, however, the vine shoot from Eden, which caused his downfall. At one and the same time, he was divinelike in his ability to re-create his world after its destruction, but very human in his frailty.

As we reflect on Noah and his potential as well as his personal struggle, we sense in ourselves our own multifarious natures. We live in the tension between the vision of our higher selves and our penchant for falling short.

Our everyday lives are fraught with our attempt to hold on to the vision of our ideal selves, which often is in conflict with our perceived selves. How do we live with such ambivalence? How can we continue to wear the garments of divine light even as we fail to learn and grow from past behavior?

Noah Returns to the Primordial State of Nakedness

We as readers cannot help but be struck by the irony that Noah, who survived the Flood and saved humanity and the world through the establishment of a covenant with God (Genesis 9:12–17), could not save himself.[8] Noah passed out in a drunken stupor, and his sons found him unconscious and completely naked (Genesis 9:21–23). In one biblical verse, Noah moved from being the master of the new earth to totally losing his standing, his dignity—his very humanity. All was lost in God's eyes as he lay prostrate in his tent. The protective divine garments seemed to have disappeared, and Noah returned to the original state of humankind: shamefully naked and vulnerable.[9]

Noah "uncovered himself [*va-yitgal*]" (Genesis 9:21) and in so doing lost the essential core of his being, the righteousness that God had recognized. Like his ancestor Adam, Noah reverted to an uncivilized state. Clothing symbolizes civility that is defined by order and rules, some of which involves privacy and modesty.

Literature is replete with examples of how clothing symbolizes society and its norms, and the removal of clothing, its demise. In the *Lord of the Flies*, written by the Nobel Prize–winning author William Golding,[10] about a group of British boys on a deserted island who attempt to govern themselves, the symbolic power of clothing has been extensively underscored. Clothing is a symbol of the world they have left behind; the removal of their clothes mirrors their discarding of civilization and descent into barbarism. The boys' preparatory school uniforms and choir robes serve to represent their innocence at the outset of the story, but as their garments turn to rags, so, too, do the rules that govern civilized behavior. Jackets and pullovers, shirts and shoes disappear as order turns to chaos. Most of the time, the boys are pictured as wearing minimal clothing and occasionally painting their bodies as well. They and their tattered garments are filthy, not only with dirt and mud, and the result of a lack of bathing, but also as a reflection of the savages they have become.

The biblical writers also utilized the images of tattered, filthy clothing to symbolize the sinfulness of individuals and nations who refused to obey the rules, in this case, God's commandments. Isaiah, for example, railed against the opponents of the prophet, who shall "wear out like a garment, the moth consuming them" (Isaiah 50:9). Similarly, Jeremiah was told to buy a beautiful linen loincloth and adorn himself with it. Then, he was instructed to bury it, then later told to dig it up. The loincloth was ruined; so, too, were the people of Israel and Judah, proclaimed God. Just as the cloth clung close to the loins of the human being, so God brought Israel close. But they would not obey, having served other gods. Therefore, they would become like the loincloth; their land would lie in ruins. Israel would be exiled to Babylonia (Jeremiah 13:1–11).

Yet, Zechariah predicted that Israel would be forgiven for its sins and would return from exile. The prophet pictured the High Priest Joshua, whose father was exiled and grandfather executed by the Babylonians, clothed in filthy garments. God ordered the removal of these clothes, symbolic of forgiving the sinfulness of the entire people that led to their destruction, and had new priestly robes placed upon him (Zechariah 3:3–5).

Changes in clothing do denote the different stages of an individual's life, and as is the case in *The Lord of the Flies*, the removal of a person's garments symbolizes the desire for freedom from constraint and the yearning for independence. In the novel

The Awakening,[11] Edna Pontellier is portrayed as being on a journey of self-discovery, and clothing—or perhaps the lack thereof—is a key symbol used by the author, Kate Chopin. Throughout the story, Edna discards more and more layers of "clothing" that inhibit her body and soul. By discarding her clothing, one item at a time, she exerts her independence. She increasingly ignores society's rules and norms. For the author, clothing represents the constraints of social behavior on women and the injustices they were forced to endure in the Victorian Age.

Like Edna, Noah, too, cast off all constraint. But in contrast, it led to his demise, just as it did to Jack, Ralph, Simon, and the other choir boys in *The Lord of the Flies.* He was cut off from God, who would never speak to him again. In a sense, he brought on his own exile (*galut*). Noah was a mere shell of himself, having become blinded to his own core identity and to the covenant that God had just established with him and his offspring, which demanded some degree of accountability for one's actions.[12] Like his predecessors, Adam and Eve, who were cut off from the Garden because of their sinfulness, Noah was now exposed by his own actions. He stood naked before God and his three sons.

Noah's actions had a lasting impact on his sons and surely carried over to future generations. Little do we know that what we do, how we act, will have a much longer-term and wider impact than we could ever imagine! In fact, the Rabbis, playing on the Hebrew root mentioned above (*galah*), stress this by picturing Noah's actions as the cause of the future exile [*galut*] of the ten tribes or perhaps the entire Jewish people.[13] So Ezekiel's castigation of Israel because of her sins, stressing that her nakedness, like Noah's, would also be exposed, resulted in her being exiled (Ezekiel 23:10). The people of Israel lost their "paradise," God's preferred place, just as the first human beings did.

Yet, Noah had been through a great deal, and it weighed heavily upon him. Surely embarrassed by the sight of their father in his drunken state, Noah's sons didn't see, and failed to understand, the pain and sorrow he carried with him as he entered the ark and embarked on his journey into a new world. To be confronted by the sight of the world as he knew it being destroyed, even as he and his family were protected on the ark that he built, to live in that cocoon for forty days amidst the cacophony, odors, and chaos of the beasts he had gathered, and finally to feel deep heartache and dread as he stepped foot on the damp soil of a devastated panorama was too much for Noah to bear. The wine enabled him to escape his pain.[14]

Witnessing Our Parents' Nakedness

Ham, Noah's second son, entered his father's tent and saw his father naked, and then told his brothers, who were outside (Genesis 9:22). How traumatic it must have been for him, and for Shem and Yaphet, to witness Noah's drunkenness, to see their father "uncovered." The sight of one's father lying naked on the floor in vomit is something that children can never forget. But seeing his nakedness was only a small part of it; his uncovering made them privy to all of his sorrow, which probably was even more devastating. How difficult it is to carry feelings of shame for our mother or father![15]

To witness a parent's imperfections, let alone a destructive act, perhaps is one of the most difficult moments for a child. When the veneer that hides a parent peels away and children see for the first time who the parent really is, this can have a damaging impact on the children and the parents they in turn might become. Perhaps we ourselves witnessed the "exposure" of a parent and it changed us forever. This may be one of the meanings that we can discern from the fact that the biblical text here identifies Ham as "the father of Canaan" (Genesis 9:22), which is expected. None of the other sons' progeny is mentioned.

Ham saw Noah drunk and naked, and his immediate reaction was to flee the tent and speak with Shem and Yaphet. How could he have reacted in any other way? Can we envision acting any differently than Ham, we who would not want to be privy to anything of the sort? And perhaps we have encountered a parent in a compromised state, and it was all that we could do to literally or symbolically run away as fast as we could.

Yet, the Rabbis emphasized that Ham should have immediately covered his father, as Shem and Yaphet did in the next verse of the story. As difficult as it might have been under the circumstances, Ham's immediate response should have been to empathize with his father and help him. By leaving Noah uncovered, Ham did not fulfill the commandment of honoring one's parent.[16]

The midrash stresses that Ham's children saw his lack of empathy for his father and the disrespect he showed him, and internalized his model, thereby also cutting themselves off from God. As a result, his descendants were pictured suffering under foreign rule and exiled from their lands. Isaiah predicted that Egypt and Nubia, two of his progeny, would be taken as captives by Assyria, carted off naked and bare (Isaiah 20:3–4).[17] Just as Ham refused to cover his father's nakedness, so, too, his children were shamed in the same manner. Of all of Ham's children, Canaan was pictured as being the most despised, perhaps because he was mentioned by name in the biblical narrative.[18]

The actions of Ham and Canaan force us to contemplate those times when we, too, were insensitive to our parents or even to our grandparents, those occasions when we showed little empathy and understanding. Perhaps in these instances we were unwilling to reach out and lessen some of the pain or indignity they felt because we were impervious to what they had experienced in their lives. These moments may still haunt us as we continue to feel the attendant guilt. In addition, we cannot avoid thinking about the models that our parents presented to us, how we learned from them and the extent to which we have internalized their behavior. We may frequently think that we are so utterly different from our parents—so much more adept and sensitive as parents to our own children. But there comes a point for many of us when we realize the extent to which we have become so much like them, and not always for the good.

Covering the Shame of Those We Love

Unlike their brother Ham, Shem and Yaphet understood what was expected of them. They knew that they had to preserve the honor of their parent, much of it symbolized by their father's garments—garments of adornment as well as protection. The literary quality of the biblical text is striking here as it describes how they acted. It is highly alliterative, thus emphasizing the importance of the cloth (in Hebrew, *simlah*) with which they covered Noah. Listen to the words: "But Shem and Yaphet took a *simlah* [cloth] and *yasimu* [placed it] on the *shechem* [backs] of *sheneihem* [both of them]" (Genesis 9:23). Similar alliteration appears two verses before, when Noah became intoxicated: "He drank [*va-yeisht*] the wine and became drunk [*va-yishkar*]" (Genesis 9:21). The extent of the repetition of the Hebrew letters *sin* and *shin* underscores the biblical writer's intention to link these two verses—to stress that the antidote to Noah's sinfulness was Shem and Yaphet's honoring of their father by covering him.[19]

How many of us believe that our actions can have a truly transformative impact on our parents, that we can help them overcome their problems? Do we feel we actually possess the power to make our parents' lives better? Still seeing ourselves as their children, can we even countenance the idea that what we do can make a difference in how they live their lives?

But there is more to our story. The two brothers not only covered their father, but they also refused to even gaze upon his nakedness, entering the tent walking backward and exiting in the same manner. They are pictured as covering their faces to ensure that they wouldn't see their father's ashen countenance.[20] Furthermore, they themselves symbolically "wore the cloth" that they used—they placed it on their shoulders as they entered their father's tent before putting it on him. They empathically placed themselves in their father's position; they literally wore his clothing, felt his shame.

Shem and Yaphet acted in a godlike manner, honoring their father by enveloping him in a protective garment. As a result, their children and future progeny learned from their model and were rewarded accordingly.[21]

The Rabbis also believed that because Shem was mentioned first, he played the decisive role in the biblical narrative. In effect, Yaphet followed his example and directions.[22] So when Nebuchadnezzer cast Shadrach, Meshach, and Abed-nego, descendants of Shem, into a fiery furnace, they were thrown in with their clothing, which was not burned and which saved them (Daniel 3:19–27). They were not only wrapped in their clothes and, therefore, never left shamefully naked, but also because their father covered his father's nakedness, they miraculously survived.[23]

Our Actions Have Far-Reaching Impact

The Rabbis, however, saw that the reward given to Shem's progeny because of their ancestor's legacy went far beyond the salvation of the three individuals thrown into the fiery furnace as described by Daniel. The Jewish people as a whole, through its covenant with God, were given the privilege of wearing the tallit, the ritual shawl, and tefillin, the phylacteries that are wrapped around the arm and head, both used during daily prayer. Jews cover themselves with these garments that affirm their people's relationship with God and ensure their place in the World to Come.[24] The descendants of Shem, who preserved his father's honor by covering him, were adorned with garments that brought majesty and ultimate glory.[25]

These very qualities are associated with the Divine at the moment of Creation, as we see in Psalms:

> "Adonai, my God, You are very great; You are clothed in glory and majesty [*hod ve-hadar*], wrapped in a garment of light. You spread the heavens like a tent cloth."
> (Psalm 104:1–2)[26]

The garments that God wears are symbolic of the essence of God's nature, as perceived through God's acts in the world. Human beings can only discern God's Presence as it is manifest in the Divine's outward garments.

Similarly, the garments worn by the descendants of Shem and by all human beings are symbolic of our inner qualities. We can be godlike when our actions manifest the divine light present from the moment of Creation. So we are forced to ask whether the garments with which we cover ourselves are really vehicles that adorn us or that suffocate us. Do they represent the best of human life, embodying that which we all strive for and hope to be? And more: do our garments represent the values of our parents and their parents, born out of their sense of how we are expected to treat other human beings, especially those closest to us?

Awakening to the Reality of What We Have Done

The end of our biblical scene is a bit unclear. We read that "when Noah awoke [*va-yiketz*] from his stupor, he knew [*va-yeida*] what his youngest son had done to him and he said, 'Cursed be Canaan'" (Genesis 9:24–25). First we note that Noah is said to have literally "awakened from his wine," not from "his sleep or stupor," which we would expect. It is as if the biblical writer emphasizes that once the wine wore off, Noah literally "put an end" (playing on *keitz* and *va-yiketz*, from the same Hebrew root) to the wine because he understood what the wine had done to him. He now is pictured as truly "knowing" (*yeida*), similar to his ancestor Adam, who ate from the Tree of Knowledge and then knew the difference between good and evil. Noah was able to recognize the actions of his sons, especially Ham's reaction to seeing him intoxicated in his tent. He, like Adam, had tasted the forbidden fruit, which resulted in the pain of knowing how evil works in the world and what it has done to his family.

But there are other difficulties at the end of our story. The biblical text focuses on Noah's three sons, of whom Ham was the middle child, so why does it now mention Noah's youngest child and what he did to him? Ham was not the youngest son. Furthermore, when Noah awakened, he said, "Cursed be Canaan" (Genesis 9:25). Why mention Canaan, the youngest of the four sons of Ham here (Genesis 10:6) and have a curse fall on one of his grandchildren?[27] Perhaps the mention of Noah's grandchild at this point serves to further underscore the impact of sinful acts upon future generations. The sins of parents may be visited upon their children. Noah's grandchild is cursed because of the fruit of the ground, a curse that Adam carried with him out of the Garden (Genesis 3:17) and now was manifested by Canaan's grandfather.

Noah was the heir to the garments worn by Adam and Eve, which represented the protection and potential of humankind. Knowing, however, involves our capacities as human beings to do both good and evil. Just as Noah and his sons were tested, the garments of Eden would continue to challenge the generations who would wear them in the future. Shem, Noah's firstborn, handed them down to Abraham, who in turn would pass them on to his progeny.[28]

3

THE GARMENTS OF DISGUISE— AM I JACOB OR ESAU?

Revealing and Concealing Identity

Genesis 27:11–27

The garments of Adam and Eve that were handed down from generation to generation never lost the sweet aroma of the Garden of Eden. Whether they were in the possession of Seth, Enoch, Methuselah, Noah, Shem, Eber, or even the wicked Nimrod, they carried with them divinelike power and the memory of paradise. When, for example, the animals and birds of Eden saw the first human beings covered in the Divine's garments, they were awestruck, and each subsequent individual who donned them was enhanced by wearing them.[1]

The Garments of the Hunter

Although most Rabbinic traditions emphasize that the garments were handed down to Abraham, who bequeathed them to Isaac, who handed them down to his firstborn son, Esau,[2] one tradition suggests that Esau stole them from Nimrod, the king of Babylonia. When the garments were in Nimrod's possession, he was a feared hunter. It was believed that the clothing had animal designs on them, which drew Nimrod's prey to him, enabling him to kill them easily.[3] Esau, himself a man of the field, coveted Nimrod's magical clothing.[4] As a result, a ferocious battle ensued between Esau and Nimrod and his men, which resulted in Esau's gaining possession of the garments from Eden.[5] Once Esau put on the divine garments, he became like Nimrod, a mighty and cunning hunter.[6]

Because the garments were a legacy from the past given to humankind by God, they had to be protected. The Rabbis generally believed that they were placed in his mother Rebecca's tent, either because Esau himself did not trust his foreign wives[7] or because his parents were concerned about the continuity of the line of Abraham.[8] Some even suggest that Jacob, after gaining the birthright from his older brother, believed that Esau no longer deserved to wear the garments, and so he took them and hid them in the ground.[9]

These traditions compel us to reflect on whether we ourselves are worthy of wearing the garments entrusted to us by previous generations. We have been bequeathed values and traditions that embody that which those who came before us believed to be worthy of preservation. We may often wonder whether we have both the insight to understand their importance and the ability to keep them intact so that we, in turn, can bequeath them to our own children.

And if we do, then we are also concerned about the extent to which our immediate families, our spouses and our children, recognize their importance. Are they moved to embrace parts of who we are, our worldviews and values? Do they manifest a desire to make our garments a part of who they are … or desire to be? Or are we deeply disappointed that our prized clothing, that which adorns our lives, is seen as unimportant, antiquated, and irrelevant to their lives? If we have cajoled and badgered them enough so that they have grudgingly taken the garments that we hold dear, do they remain hidden in the bottom of one of their drawers, never to be worn?

Esau's Garments: The Source of Blessing or the Means of Trickery?

We already have come to understand that clothing represents more than superficial covering; it reveals the identity of the one who wears it. So it was with the garments utilized by Rebecca to disguise Jacob in our story. They were laden with deeper meaning and insight into the complex nature of Isaac's sons, Esau and Jacob, and how he and Rebecca related to them.

When Isaac grew old, he asked Esau, the one who provided the family with food, to hunt for game and then prepare his favorite dish. In return, he would give him the blessing as the firstborn in the family (Genesis 27:1–4). Rebecca, having overheard Isaac's request, but also being privy to the oracle's prediction that Jacob would be the primary heir to Isaac (Genesis 25:22–23), instructed Jacob on how to usurp the blessing and thereby guarantee his future. She told him to fetch two choice young goats, which she would cook. He then would bring the food to his almost blind father, who, thinking he was Esau, would bless him (Genesis 27:5–13).

Jacob was incredulous. How could he possibly accomplish this? After all, his brother was hairy, and he was smooth-skinned; if his father touched him, he would see him as a trickster (Genesis 27:11–12). How could Jacob disguise his own identity or, more, assume the identity of Esau and get away with this ruse?

The difficulty of acting as someone else, especially when you are so utterly different from that person, is underscored when a character plays the role of someone else in a book, movie, or play. A movie released recently, *The Devil's Double*, based on a book written by Latif Yahia, an Iraqi-born author, PhD in international law, and former military officer in the Iraqi army, tells how he was forcibly recruited to be the body double of Saddam Hussein's eldest son, Uday Hussein. He was expected to make public appearances in the guise of Uday whenever dangerous situations arose. He was trained to imitate Uday's speech patterns and mannerisms, and he underwent surgery and dental work to make their appearances more similar.

Latif was played in the movie by Dominic Cooper, who received rave reviews for his ability to portray two characters who were so totally different from one another. Uday was a psychopath who arbitrarily tortured and killed people, a dictator's son who fulfilled every desire he had for power, wealth, and women. And he would stop at nothing to do so. Latif, on the other hand, was a bright, devoted family person whose greatest fear was that his family would be killed if he did not comply with Hussein's wishes. Reviewers noted the difficulty of "playing" such different roles, a real-life sadistic murderer and the poor sap ordered to be his stand-in.[10]

Jacob understood how different Esau was from him, and not only by virtue of Esau's hairy body. In many older cultures, long hair symbolized strength and fertility. In the Bible, Samson may be the best example of a character whose strength was dependent on his not cutting his hair. In ancient Greece, long hair on men was a symbol of power and wealth, while a shaven head was fitting for a slave. Several Greek gods possessed long hair, including Zeus, Achilles, Apollo, and Poseidon, and Greek soldiers usually wore their hair long in battle. In the Middle Ages in Europe, long hair was often the style of free men, while shorter hair signified servitude and peasantry. In Ireland, English colonists who wore their hair long signaled their rejection of their role as English subjects. Irishmen showed their strength and independence by wearing long hair.[11]

Given the symbolism of long hair, the question that Jacob had to ask himself was how he could literarily and figuratively "cover" himself? Clothing has always been a way to disguise identity, both for royalty and for commoners. Even King Saul in the Bible disguised himself by wearing different garments when he visited the witch of En-dor who summoned up the ghost of Samuel (1 Samuel 28:8). Unbeknownst to Saul, however, when he donned these garments, he himself essentially was changed.[12] Reminiscent of Jacob feigning to be his brother, Zechariah noted that individuals often disguised themselves with a hairy mantle (Zechariah 13:4–5).

In our story, we learn that Rebecca, after preparing the food to be brought to Isaac, first placed goatskins on Jacob's hairless arms and neck (Genesis 27:16). Rebecca had to work on the animal skins in order to make them fit Jacob. They had to be sewn together to fit Jacob's body, just as Eve had sewn the fig leaves and God had made garments from skins in the Garden. And since nothing was more pungent than skins from a freshly killed goat, Rebecca had to work extensively on the skins to make them resemble the odor of Esau's body. Through her work, she transformed the skins into garments that would enable Jacob to fool his father's sense of smell and touch.[13]

Hopefully, we also understand that for particular garments to fit us correctly, they often need to be altered. We must make the garments—the qualities and values—we inherit fit us if they are to enhance us. They must reflect who we are at our core, but this demands that we have a clear sense of our essential natures.

But Rebecca took even greater precautions. She also used Esau's special clothes, his *bigdei chamudot* (Genesis 27:15), which she kept with her, and dressed Jacob. These clothes, identified as the very garments worn by Adam and Eve, were now going to be worn by Jacob as part of the ruse to obtain his father's blessing.

Yet, clothing can be used to adorn and enhance the individuals who wear it, not only to mask their true intentions. It may bring out people's best qualities, not merely enable them to hurt others and diminish themselves.

Some say that Esau's special garments were kept in Rebecca's possession because Esau wore them when he tended to his father, Isaac.[14] He only wore the divine garments inherited from previous generations, the best clothing that he possessed, when he served Isaac. In so doing, Esau, of all the biblical characters, was seen as the exemplar of *kibbud av*, honoring one's parent, because he wore royal garments in his father's presence, garments that were readily available at a moment's notice.[15]

The garments we choose to wear often reflect our attitudes toward those with whom we associate, the value we place on these relationships as well as on our essential natures. Esau, who was the proverbial caregiver for his father and the one who provided the family with food, nevertheless was able to continually serve Isaac with a sense of honor and respect. We who have played these roles know how hard it sometimes is to say, *Hineini*, "Here I am [ready to act]," as Esau did when Isaac called out, *Beni*, "My son" (Genesis 27:1), expecting that Esau would do his bidding one more time. He may not have reciprocated his father's call of "My son" with his own, *Hineini Avi*, "Here I am, my father," but he did respond, albeit in a curt and less affectionate manner.

When our aging parent calls again and again, what is our initial response? How ready and willing are we to extend ourselves as caregivers when others in our immediate family are rarely called upon? Donning garments of honor, as Esau does, even if done grudgingly, is sometimes difficult for every son or daughter caring for a parent who depends on them.

The famous Rabbinic figure Rabban Shimon ben Gamaliel is said to have commented, "I honored my father all my life, but I never did even a hundredth of what Esau did. When I brought him food, washed him, or cleaned his house, I put on my oldest clothes, so as not to soil my good garments. Then, when I left and went out to the street, I changed into my good clothes. Esau, on the other hand, put on his most precious garments when he served Isaac. He felt it was only proper to wear royal garments to serve one's father." These garments were handed down from the Garden of Eden and were the very garments that would appropriately lead to the blessing that Isaac would confer on his son.[16] The son who honors his father by continually serving him and treating him as royalty surely deserved to be blessed.

According to this tradition, the royal garments worn by Esau in the service of his father present him as being enveloped by God's Presence, just as the kings of Judah and Israel and many of the prophets. They were frequently portrayed as wearing *bigdei chamudot*, precious garments like Esau's that embodied God's spirit and majesty and signified the individual's willingness to act on behalf of others and the larger community.[17]

The Person Makes the Clothes

The notion that the fragrance of Esau and his garments was that of the fields coheres with Isaac's comment when he blessed Jacob: "[Isaac] smelled his clothes and he blessed him, saying, 'See, the smell of my son is like the smell of the fields that Adonai has blessed'" (Genesis 27:27). Jacob entered Isaac's presence wearing the goatskins, but Esau's clothes carried with them the scent of Eden.[18] After all, these were the garments worn by Adam and Eve in the Garden, which is identified with the fields as well as with the Temple Mount. Some Rabbis, therefore, suggest that the scent of Esau's garments was reminiscent of the *rei'ach nicho'ach*, the fragrance of the spices used in the Temple sacrifices.[19]

However, the Rabbis argue whether it was indeed the garments themselves that bore the smell of Eden or whether the sweet fragrance was the product of the person wearing them, making them pleasing to both Isaac and God. For some, the issue was not the actual garments, but rather the identity and character of the wearer. A few commentators suggested that it was not only the sweet smell of the garments worn by Esau but also Esau himself who was a delight to Isaac's soul![20]

Yet, because Jacob represented the continuity of the chosen line, most argue that the odor pleasing to God, the *rei'ach nicho'ach*, was the *ru'ach nicho'ach*, the pleasing spirit/soul of Jacob. When Jacob donned Esau's garments, he in effect consecrated them,[21] because he carried with him the sweet scent of Eden. In contrast, when Esau entered his father's tent, *geihinnom* (hell) entered with him, but Jacob was accompanied by paradise.[22]

From these perspectives, the actual garments are neutral; they bear no positive or negative connotation of good or evil. Their impact and importance depend on the individuals who wear them, the values they possess as they fulfill their roles. The clothes do not make the person; at most, they enhance his or her character. The person and his or her essential nature fill out the garments worn.

This is made even clearer when some Rabbinic comments focus on the actual wording of the key verse, "And [Isaac] smelled his clothes." The word in Hebrew for "his clothes," *begadav*, could be read as *bogedav*, because the Rabbis were reading an unvocalized text. (The vocalization pattern was not fixed until the seventh to eighth century by the Masoretes, and in our focused word, the Hebrew consonants are the same.) The word pronounced *bogedav* means "his traitors."[23] According to this reading, Isaac saw through Jacob's disguise and realized his treachery, perhaps his essential makeup. The garments he wore revealed his true identity, which would have an impact on future generations.

Garments Can Reveal/Conceal Identity

From the very outset of our story, the key issue is the core identity of the characters, including Isaac, the family patriarch. Although he appeared to be blind, based upon the dialogue and questions he asked in the story, we the readers might wonder whether he actually saw through the ruse and was willingly complicit.

The essential identities of the two obvious pairs of actors on the surface could not be more different: Isaac was blind and passive, while Rebbeca was seen as the one who managed what transpired from behind the scenes.[24] Jacob was smooth-skinned and a stay-at-home, but his brother was a hunter and was hairy all over.

However, our understanding of these characters may not reflect how they always were. Individuals can change over time, and perhaps we see this in Rebecca from the time she initially encountered Isaac until the birth of her twins twenty years later.

When Abraham's servant Eliezer brought Rebecca back from Laban's house in Aram Naharaim to marry Isaac, the very first time she set eyes on him, she said, "Who is this man walking in the field toward us?" (Genesis 24:65). Isaac is described by the Rabbis as meditating or praying at that moment, based on the biblical writer's choice of words: "He went out walking [*la-suach*] in the field" (Genesis 24:63). The word for "walking" here is not the usual *la-lechet*. Seeing Isaac in a heightened spiritual state, Rebecca was overwhelmed and literally fell off the camel (Genesis 24:64). Aviva Zornberg suggests that Rebecca saw "a vital anguish at the heart of [Isaac's] prayers," and she was overwhelmed by him. The near-death experience of the *Akeidah* (the Binding of Isaac) had shaped his essential makeup.[25]

When Eliezer responded, "This is my master," Rebecca was at a total loss for words. In fact, we do not hear her voice again for twenty years. Yet, her deep-seated feelings were expressed by her actions: "She took her veil and covered herself" (Genesis 24:65). The act of putting on a veil can serve many purposes and convey much about the individual. Although most Rabbinic commentators see this as a sign of Rebecca's modesty,[26] some go further, suggesting that Rebecca was overcome with fear and trepidation upon seeing Isaac's intensity and spiritual fervor. She lost all confidence that she was worthy of being his wife. Fearful of revealing her conflict and doubts, she masked herself, hiding her innermost feelings. In effect, she disappeared, became "other."[27]

Many of us also have donned a veil in order to hide from others and perhaps to escape taking responsibility for our own lives. Whether the veil is self-deprecation ("I cannot possibly do that!" "I don't have the ability or the wherewithal to move in a new direction!"), debilitating fear, or procrastination, among many possibilities, it is used to ensure that we will never fail, but concomitantly never grow. And once the veil is in place, it seems to be such an integral part of our being that we cannot see ourselves clearly, just as others do not take notice of us.

It is only when Rebecca conceived Esau and Jacob that her silence was broken with an existential cry of pain during her pregnancy, "If so, why do I exist?" (Genesis 25:22). Esau and Jacob struggled (*va-yitrotzatzu*) in her womb, and she herself was torn apart (*ratzatz*).[28] Yet, it is through personal struggle that Rebecca began to take responsibility for her life and for her actions and, in so doing, lifted the veils from herself. She confronted her anguish and despair and embarked on a journey to find meaning in her life. A dynamic force was unleashed that would lead to a radically different sense of herself, and all this came as a result of her pregnancy.[29]

Rebecca was no longer hidden, submerged, other, but rather had begun to embrace her own strength and become whole. She overcame her awe of Isaac, who himself grew older and seemingly more feeble, and she became a force in the patriarchal family.[30]

To recognize the essential makeup of the characters, especially as they change, is difficult enough, but when they are camouflaged, it is even more of a challenge. Jacob, feigning to be his brother, was covered with goatskins that were prepared to simulate Esau's hairy body and confuse his father.

Interestingly, hair itself is a body covering that can also represent ambiguity: it is part of one's body and at the same time external to it; it emanates from within and can beautify, but also can symbolize the animalistic and even the demonic in us (as opposed to smoothness, which signifies simplicity as well as a lack of depth).[31]

When Isaac was confronted by Jacob, who brought him his food in anticipation of receiving the blessing, the ambiguity and obfuscation led Isaac to focus on the key issue of the entire narrative. When Jacob entered the tent, he called out, "My father [*avi*]," and Isaac responded with the classic word *Hineini* ("Here I am"), but then unexpectedly added, "Who are you, my son?"—in Hebrew, *Mi atah beni* (Genesis 27:18). Isaac asked the very same question of Esau when he subsequently returned from the field with the game he had killed—*Mi atah*, "Who are you?" (Genesis 27:32)—thus underscoring for us as readers the essential concern about identity that was at stake. If we countenance the possibility that Isaac knew it was Jacob in front of him, then the question is even more poignant—Isaac as a parent was willing to challenge his son, forcing him to confront himself—who he was, who he had become!

Have we who have been blessed to be parents been strong enough to dare risk challenging our children in this way? Do we even want to hear the answers to such questions? And even if Isaac truly didn't recognize Jacob, the question still must have resonated in the deepest recesses of his son's soul as he then responded, claiming to be the other: "I am Esau, your firstborn" (Genesis 27:19).

What is most apparent and inescapable in the interchanges between Isaac and his sons is a real confusion of identity. No fewer than four times Isaac asked both Jacob and Esau some version of the question "Who are you?" Even after Isaac blessed Jacob, he nevertheless still had the question of his identity in mind and asked him directly, but in a most ambiguous way, "*Atah zeh beni Eisav*," which if translated literally should read, "Are you this one, my son Esau?" And the confusion of the true identity of this son is heightened by Jacob's reply, "*Ani*," meaning "I" (Genesis 27:24). What can this possibly mean? Was he really Jacob, or had he taken on both the characteristics and the place of his brother?

Jacob's own confusion about his identity is palpable in the narrative, and the change of clothing both heightens the confusion and symbolizes it. Similarly, in *Gulliver's Travels*, the author, Jonathan Swift, uses clothing to raise questions about the character's identity. Gulliver pays extraordinary attention to his clothes throughout his journeys, always describing his garments in detail. His journey from England into new cultures is a journey into new clothing. But the clothing motif carries a deeper, more psychological meaning. Gulliver's concern about his clothes may signal a deep-seated anxiety about his own identity, because he is refashioned in all the places he ventures to. He seems to lose a sense of who he essentially is. Significantly, the two moments when he is described as being naked—when he is the boy toy of the Brodingnagian maids and when he is assaulted by a Yahoo girl as he bathes—suggest more than his prudishness. Gulliver associates nakedness with his extreme vulnerability and how nonexistent he really feels.[32]

And it was the clothing that Jacob was wearing—Esau's garments and the goatskins—that also then led to Isaac's confusion about Jacob's identity. He concluded, "The voice is the voice of Jacob, but the hands are the hands of Esau," and as a result, "he did not recognize him" (Genesis 27:22–23). For Isaac and for us, the issue is not only whether it was Jacob or Esau who was standing before Isaac, but also the seemingly conflicted identity of Jacob himself. The clothing representing Esau was worn by Jacob, or perhaps it had become a part of him!

To expand one's individual, unique identity and take on the characteristics of another is ultimately to blur the differences between you and the other.[33] When Jacob put on the animal skins to pass for Esau, he took on Esau's essential nature—his masculinity and his power. He has been described as a kind of cross-dresser who was enhanced by special garments to overcome his feminized family position. Jacob was seen as a man in drag enacting his newly acquired masculinity.[34] In acquiring the birthright and usurping the blessing, he became in part Edom and Seir, the ruddy, hairy Esau, full of powerful energy and highly charged sexuality.

In putting on Esau's garments, he was perhaps not merely dressing himself up as another. Impersonation is an expression of the desire to expand the breadth of one's own identity, to become more complex.[35] Jacob now "revealed" to his father his own more differentiated nature. He was not a copy of Isaac, mild and somewhat passive, but one who was capable of taking action, of leading.[36]

Simply put, Jacob spoke the truth when he said, in response to Isaac, "I am Esau, your firstborn" (Genesis 27:19). He now embodied a different sense of himself and his destiny. Jacob gained strength from this seeming act of trickery. It is as if he earned his father's blessing.[37] Of course, Isaac was not sure who the son was whom he blessed, even after blessing him. The voice was indeed that of Jacob, while the hands were the hands of Esau. Jacob now projected a much more complex and stronger identity, which melded the important qualities of his father and grandfather, Abraham. Perhaps all of this was the prerequisite for assuming the role of patriarch of the family.

One can almost picture Jacob's subsequent musings:

"At first, when my mother placed the animal skins on my arms and neck, and I put on Esau's clothes, I felt very strange. Nothing seemed to fit. The skins kept sliding off my arms, and I kept scratching my neck. I felt it just wasn't right to disguise myself as my brother. And besides, father would surely be able to tell the difference between the costume I was wearing and my brother's true nature. And he would then curse me instead of blessing me.

"But soon I began to feel more comfortable. It was almost as if the clothes and the skins were meant for me. A strange sensation overcame me—it was as if a part of me that had been there, dormant all along, had now emerged. I felt as if a side of me had awakened at that moment. So when I carried the food mother had prepared into my father's tent, and he reacted by saying,

'Who are you, my son?' it seemed almost natural for me to say, without thinking, 'I am Esau, your firstborn.' At that moment, I truly felt like my brother."[38]

"See, the Smell of My Son"

The situation must have been so confusing for Isaac. How would he be able to discern which son stood before him? To do so, he was forced to utilize each of his senses. After straining unsuccessfully to make out the image of the person, he was forced to ask, "Who are you, my son?" He heard his son's voice, but he yet insisted that Jacob come close so he could feel him. Nevertheless, he was still confused. The voice was surely Jacob's, but the feel of his hands and neck gave Isaac pause: they seemed hairy like Esau. He then asked to taste the food that his son hunted and prepared for him, knowing that Esau would bring wild game. However, the actual taste of the food that Jacob presented was very different, because it was meat that Rebecca had cooked using the two young goats from the pen near the house. Finally, Isaac asked Jacob to draw even closer so that he could kiss him and, in so doing, take in his unique smells and those of his garments (Genesis 27:18–27).

The confusion of the moment is underscored by the language used by Isaac after attempting to know whom he was blessing. After resorting to all his senses—he heard, touched, tasted, and smelled—he then cried out, "See [re'eh]! The smell of my son is like the smell of the fields that Adonai has blessed" (Genesis 27:27). The sense of confusion is quite evident, but it led to a deeper knowledge of the son he was holding in his arms. As he smelled the goatskins and the garments Jacob was wearing, he experienced a moment of enlightenment. (The Jewish Publication Society translates re'eh as simply "Ah!" This is, from our modern perspective, an "aha" moment.) What Isaac finally sensed was not the foul-smelling goatskins, but rather Esau's garments that were worn by Adam and Eve in the Garden and were handed down through the generations, which now adorned Jacob. They, indeed, bore the smell of the fields that God blessed in the Creation. (There is even the notion that this alludes to the fields of apple trees of Eden.[39]) Jacob carried with him the blessing of the past, intimations of paradise even in the imperfect world outside the Garden, even in a world of deception.[40]

But notice the powerful choice of words used by the biblical writer here. Isaac did not say, "See, the smell of my son's garments." Rather, he said, "See, the smell of *my son*"! The garments merely represented those who wore them. Isaac now understood that it was ultimately the essence of Jacob that would transmit the potential of perfection to his progeny, the pleasing scent of righteousness.[41] In a sense, it was only when Jacob wore the garments that they carried the aroma of Eden. It was Jacob who had the potential to bring blessing.[42] Jacob was transformed when he dressed as Esau, when he donned the garments from paradise. Jacob now was adorned by a new and enriched self, which would ensure blessing. It would bring the dew of heaven upon him and his people in the time to come (Genesis 27:28).

Isaac's emphasis on the word *beni*, "[the smell of] my son," led to many Rabbinic interpretations over the centuries. However, one escaped the eyes of most of the commentators and midrashim: the play on *beni* and *benoi*. *Noi* in Hebrew means "pleasantness," "sweetness," even "goodness." Read in this way, the Genesis 27:27 passage could mean, "He blessed him, saying, 'See, the sweet smell." Jacob, not his garments, carried the *rei'ach nicho'ach*, the sweet aroma reminiscent of the smells of the sacrifices in the Temple in Jerusalem, which one day would be rebuilt (*banui*) by the heirs to Jacob's divine garments.[43]

But which of Jacob's twelve sons would wear the divine garments of Eden? Which would transmit the potential of perfection of the Garden and preserve it for future generations? If tradition holds sway, we would expect that Jacob would bequeath the divine garment given to Adam and Eve to Reuven, his firstborn son, the son of Leah.

4
STRIPPING JOSEPH OF HIS SPECIAL COAT

A Symbol of Power and Status, a Source of Pain and Isolation

Genesis 37:3, 37:23, 37:31–33

At the urging of his mother, Rebecca, who had heard that Esau threatened to kill him once their father Isaac died, Jacob fled to Paddan-aram and Rebecca's family home (Genesis 27:41–45). Jacob carried with him both the memories of the deception and all that had transpired in its aftermath, as well as the garment that his mother had placed upon him when he received Isaac's blessing.

The special garment, which had been Esau's and was preserved by Rebecca, gave off the aroma of Eden and therefore was precious to Jacob. It reminded him of his beloved mother and of the blessing by his father, which embodied links to his people's past and their hope for the future.

The Focus on the Garment in Jacob's Family

During the entire twenty years he served Laban, his mother's brother in Haran, Jacob preserved the coat and the threads of memory woven into it.

On occasion he took it out and looked at it in the secrecy of his tent to remind himself of the home from which he was forced to flee, but also perhaps to remain aware of the scars he suffered when he inherited the divine promise made to his ancestors. He even placed the garment on his shoulders, as if to reassure himself that he was worthy of carrying forward the promise and the hope of his people.[1]

It is not unlike the times when we find ourselves rummaging through the remnants of our childhood that have been stored away in attic trunks for safekeeping. Many of them bear not only fond memories of times we spent within our extended families, especially in family celebrations that shaped in part who we have become, but also painful moments of isolation, anger, and loss.

Jacob also understood that it was most appropriate to take out the coat and use it to celebrate special times in the life of his family and his people. One such moment was his wedding night with the youngest of Laban's daughters, his cousin, Rachel. He gave Rachel his mother's coat to wear, not only sealing their bond but also tying them to their people's past and seeding its future. The coat symbolized Jacob's relationship with Rachel, for whom he had labored in Laban's house for seven years after falling in love with her the very first time he gazed upon her. He eagerly enveloped her in his special coat, in which she appeared incomparably beautiful.[2]

Laban, however, deceived Jacob by substituting his daughter Leah under the cover of darkness and hidden by the splendid coat that she now wore. The precious garment, taken from Rachel and hidden in a secret chest by Laban,[3] was used to disguise the identity of Laban's firstborn daughter rather than celebrating Jacob's love for Rachel. As a result, Jacob would now have to work an additional seven years until he could marry Rachel (Genesis 29:22–28). Although it is not clear what, if any, affection Jacob possessed for Leah (Genesis 29:31),[4] she did become the mother of six of his progeny, representing half of the future twelve tribes of Israel. The magical garment handed down from Adam and Eve, therefore, enhanced the moment of inception of Jacob's family and the birthing of the nation.

After seven frustrating years of waiting, Jacob married Rachel, who was bedecked in the very same divine garment that she wore seven years before in anticipation of initially marrying Jacob. Everyone in the family thereafter referred to it as "Rachel's *kutonet passim*," her "striped garment."[5] It was, therefore, not surprising years later, after Rachel died in childbirth (Genesis 35:16–19), that the divine garment would be given to one of her sons.

Knowing the history of the garment, we would have presumed that its rightful heir would have been Reuben, Jacob's firstborn, the son of Leah. However, the Rabbis believed that because Reuben had the audacity to sleep with Bilhah, his father's concubine (Genesis 35:22), he lost his rights to the garment, which symbolized respect, authority, royalty, and wisdom. Of course, one might say that the coat should then have been bequeathed to one of the next sons in line, one of Leah's sons—Shimon, Levi, or Judah. Yet, the counterargument surely was that since Leah's firstborn son abdicated his position by virtue of his sin, it should be given to Rachel's firstborn, Joseph.

As the years passed, Jacob's special love for Joseph became evident to the entire family, especially to Joseph's eleven brothers. When Joseph matured, already tending the flocks at the age of seventeen, Jacob gave him the coat that had been in the possession of his mother. In so doing, the divine garment would always remind Jacob of his beloved Rachel.

The striped garment, handed down through the generations and now worn by Rachel's firstborn son, would serve as a marker for Joseph's entire life journey. From his youth, when his brothers ripped his garment from him and cast him into the pit to eventually sell him to the caravan heading to Egypt, to his confrontation with the wife of his Egyptian master, Potiphar, to his becoming viceroy of Egypt, his garment was a symbol of who he was at each stage of his life.

In a similar manner, many classic novels utilize garments to trace the evolution of the main characters. Such is the case in Zora Neale Hurston's work, *Their Eyes Were Watching God*, perhaps the best-known work by an African American writer.[6] It tells the life story of Janie Crawford, divided into three major periods corresponding to her marriages to three very different men. Through these chapters in her life, her clothing is a visual bookmark of where she is in her search for meaning and true love. Janie is first married to Logan Tilliks, an older man who simply wants a domestic helper. When she leaves Tillik's house, she discards her apron, the symbol of her servitude, in a bush alongside of the road as she picks up flowers and makes a bouquet for herself. She runs off with Jody (Joe) Starks to Eatonville, where he is only interested in gaining wealth and power, and all that he wants of Janie is to be the perfect, loving wife to reinforce his position in the town. In his jealousy, he makes Janie wear a head rag to cover her beautiful hair so that no other men would be attracted to her. After Starks dies, she has considerable assets and is pursued by several suitors who have fine occupations. However, she falls in love with a drifter who goes by the name of Tea Cake, and they relocate to Florida to find work planting and harvesting beans. She has found her real love and does not mind working in the muck with her husband. She is pictured wearing blue denim overalls and heavy work shoes, which symbolize the time in her life in which she has found her true self.[7]

Kutonet Passim: What's in a Name?

Scholars for centuries have attempted to understand why Joseph's coat is called a *kutonet passim* in Hebrew (Genesis 37:3), and many of the ideas proffered are reflected in the various ways it has been translated over time.[8] *Kutonet* means "garment" or "coat," but what does *passim* convey? *Pas* in Hebrew means "stripe," "band," "bar," or "line," thus the sense that it was a striped or colored coat.

However, the Rabbis as well as modern biblical scholars dig deeper into the possible symbolism of the word *passim* to understand its significance. Focusing on its letters and syllables, they offer several interesting meanings for Joseph's coat. Some think of it as a painted or an ornamented cloth made of fine wool.[9] This perhaps emanated from the tradition that the coat, which was worn by Nimrod and subsequently was in the possession of Esau, was painted with pictures of animals, which gave it magical powers. Others felt that it was a long robe that covered the arms and legs, a tunic extending to the extremities. This was based on the Hebrew word *pisah*, which is used to refer to the palms and the soles of the feet.[10] Its length, as well as its possible colors or stripes, made the garment as well as Joseph stand out, thereby establishing his unique position in Jacob's family, which only embittered his brothers even more.

Joseph's garment and the reactions of his brothers to it force each of us to consider the unique garments we wear that may have led to tension with our own siblings. For some of us, it may be the unique qualities we possess as the firstborn child that became the measuring rod for our brothers and sisters, causing extreme resentment; for others of us, perhaps it was the close proximity to our parents that was a source of jealousy. Whatever it might have been, it surely caused our parents much pain, as Joseph's actions and his brother's hatred caused Jacob.

The sons of Leah, and even those of the two concubines, Bilhah and Zilpah, indeed came to hate Joseph (Genesis 37:3–4). It did not help that the special coat only served to enhance his good looks and made him resemble his mother Rachel. To the brothers, it was an anathema in every way—Joseph had usurped their position of authority and their father's love. But to Jacob, it seemed that he was always in the presence of his deceased wife. He luxuriated in Joseph's radiance; the light of Eden always surrounded him.[11]

Joseph alienated his brothers even more by the way he acted in the fields as they shepherded their father's sheep; he behaved as if he could lord it over them, "lead" them as it were.[12] And he was all of seventeen. He constantly told them what to do and how to act. What made matters worse, he frequently gossiped behind their backs. He returned from the fields filled with tales about what they had said about their father to ingratiate himself even more with Jacob.[13] In spite of Joseph's actions, or perhaps because of them, Jacob came to love Rachel's son inordinately, and he set him apart from his brothers by giving him the ornamented tunic.

The brothers grew more and more jealous of Joseph, but the breaking point came with Joseph's outlandish dreams of superiority, which he readily shared with them. He envisioned their sheaves bowing down to his sheaf, and worse, the sun, moon, and eleven stars all bowing down to him (Genesis 37:5–11), giving his siblings a clear picture of Joseph ruling over them. Joseph, for his part, seemed oblivious to how his words and actions and the coat he inherited galvanized the emotions of his brothers.

Joseph was so caught up in his dreams of grandeur that he simply could not see the extent to which all the brothers were aligned against him. Although Joseph now wore the beautiful coat of splendid colors, which symbolized his assuming his rightful place as the inheritor of Jacob's birthright, it simply masked his feelings of aloneness and vulnerability after his mother Rachel's death. The beauty of the coat and his fanciful dreams could not hide the isolation and pain he felt.

In classic literature, many characters don new clothing to assume a different appearance. For example, in Shakespeare's comedy *The Taming of the Shrew*, many of the main characters purposefully change their clothing: Sly dresses as a lord, Lucentio dresses as a Latin tutor, Tranio dresses as Lucentio, Hortensio puts on the garments of a music tutor, and the pendant dresses as Vincentio. These disguises enable the characters to transcend their social position and class and, for the first time, feel successful. But Shakespeare raises the question of whether the clothes can indeed make the man—whether a person can essentially change by putting on new garments. The ultimate answer, of course, is no; a person's true identity will always come out, no matter how differently he or she is clothed. As Petruchio implies on his wedding day, sometimes a garment is simply a garment, and the person beneath remains the same.[14]

The story of Joseph is the story of brothers or sisters who are disliked by all other siblings because their insecurity causes them to be boastful, loud, demanding, and generally obnoxious. It is someone many of us may be acquainted with. It might be one of our own brothers or sisters, who was the bane of the existence of our entire family when we were growing up, or worse, it might be one of our own children. There is a Joseph in most of our families.[15]

And just as in the case of some of our families, such animosity among Jacob's sons had terrible consequences. Joseph's possession of the coat led to his brothers throwing him into the pit and subsequently selling him for twenty pieces of silver to merchants who took him to Egypt and, in turn, sold him to Potiphar, the chief steward of Pharaoh (Genesis 39:1). According to one tradition, the coat itself, the *kutonet passim*, the cause of Joseph's suffering, already conveyed through its name the long-term impact it would have. The Hebrew letters of *passim* were taken in several midrashim to represent the names of all those who participated in the sale of Joseph and his transference to Egypt: the merchants, the Ishmaelites, the Midianites, and Potiphar himself.[16] Like the garment worn by Noah after the Flood, Joseph's divine coat had the power to cause pain if not worn with wise purpose. Similarly, our qualities, if not used wisely, can cause hurt and irreparable damage to our relationships.

We know that the coat eventually led Joseph to Egypt, which would in the future become a place in which the progeny of Jacob's sons would be enslaved for four hundred years. Yet, it also was the place in which the Jewish people were born. The ultimate redemption of Israel from Egypt and their crossing the Red Sea, which began their journey through the desert to Mount Sinai and then toward the Promised Land, was also associated with Joseph's coat. The Rabbis emphasized this by dividing the word *passim* into its two syllables, which could be read as *pas yam* in Hebrew, meaning "the cleft of the sea," that is, the division of the Red Sea. Reading the name of Joseph's coat in this way, one could say that the redemption from Egypt also occurred due to the merit of Joseph and his coat.[17]

The Coat and All Its Symbolism

There was indeed a great deal of ambivalence associated with Joseph's coat in the Rabbinic tradition. Although the coat was the cause of his being separated from his family and his people, it also was said that Joseph wore this very garment when he served Jacob. Ironically, like his uncle Esau before him, he served his father wearing a garment of honor; his special garment was worthy of honoring one's parent.[18] Although the coat would bring much pain to Jacob because it tore apart his family, nevertheless, it also represented his and his son's position of authority, which demanded respect.

The only other place in the Bible where the *kutonet passim* is mentioned comes in 2 Samuel, where Tamar, the daughter of King David, is described as wearing a similar ornamented tunic, which was a sign of royalty (2 Samuel 13:18). The midrashim even describe the coat as being purple, a key sign of royal position.[19]

Joseph was intended to be the leader of the family, and his coat symbolized his newly acquired position of authority and power. In the Bible, when an individual was elevated to kingship, he was often given distinctive clothing as the sign of his stature and newfound authority. In the book of Isaiah, for example, the transference of power is described in the following typical manner: "I will invest him with your tunic [*kutonet*], gird him with your sash, and deliver your authority into his hand; and he shall be like a father to the inhabitants of Jerusalem and the men of Judah" (Isaiah 22:21).[20] Similarly, during Babylonian rule over Israel, when the king of Babylon released Jehoiachin, the king of Judah, from prison and restored him to the throne, he changed his clothing, placing his royal garments upon him (2 Kings 25:27–29). Conversely, when authority and power were removed, it often was depicted by the tearing of one's garment.[21]

In the Rabbinic tradition, Joseph's *kutonet passim* was not only described as a royal garment of kingship, but it was also often thought of as a majestic priestly garment. Some say that it resembled the garment worn by the High Priest.[22] Either way, it was a symbol of Joseph's power and authority, which was thrust upon him at a very young age.

How ironic it is that the coat he wore would anticipate, or perhaps even eventuate in Joseph's assuming the position of viceroy of Egypt! The Pharaoh then designated Joseph's newly acquired authority by changing his garments, placing his own signet ring on his hand, and dressing him in robes of fine linen. Linen was only worn by royalty and the priesthood (Genesis 41:14, 41:42).[23]

With this in mind, it was inevitable that when the brothers first saw Joseph's regal coat, with all that it symbolized, they would come to envy and hate him even more than they already did. It wasn't enough that he primped and preened before them, penciling his eyes and curling his hair, which caused them consternation,[24] but now he bedecked himself with the symbol of their father's love for him.

When we read the biblical account, it seems that Joseph was entirely oblivious to how the brothers felt toward him and how his actions exacerbated their feelings. However, perhaps Joseph recognized his brothers' feelings more than we, the readers, might think. So, as he journeyed at the behest of his father to Shechem to join them with the flocks in pasture (Genesis 37:12–14), he might have been concerned about appearing in his divine coat. Therefore, according to one tradition, he attempted to cover the coat with another outward garment so they would not see it.[25]

Are we any different than Joseph? We, too, are sometimes torn between flaunting our "special garments," whether they are actual clothing or the symbols of our achievements, to underscore our importance in the eyes of others, on the one hand, and concealing them so that we can be perceived to be "one of them," on the other. We also occasionally downplay things about ourselves so as not to set ourselves apart, including what we possess or things we have done.

Removing the Mask of Both Joseph and His Brothers

The tradition that Joseph was wearing more than one garment when he went to see his brothers is based on the Bible saying that the brothers "stripped Joseph of his tunic [*kutonto*], the ornamented tunic [*kutonet ha-passim*] he was wearing" (Genesis 37:23). The apparent redundancy in this verse and the use of different terms—the *kutonet passim* is only mentioned once—led the Rabbis to speculate that Joseph was wearing at least two, but perhaps as many as four different garments.[26] If this were the case, the intent of the brothers seems to have been to strip Joseph bare of all that covered him, even his undergarments.[27]

As the brothers were tearing the coat and other garments from him, Joseph attempted in vain to protect the coat. Listen to Thomas Mann's reimagining of the scene at the pit:

> To [Joseph], the most terrible ... thing of all was what happened to the *kutonet....* Desperately he tried to protect the garment and to keep the remnant and ruins of it still upon him. Several times he cried out: "My coat! My coat!" and even after he stood naked [in front of them], he still begged them ... to spare it. Yes, he was naked ... the coat, shift, and loincloth ... lay in tatters.[28]

We as readers understand why Joseph struggled to protect the special coat. The coat, which was his mother's, Jacob having bequeathed it to him, enabled him to overcome his feelings of aloneness after Rachel's death. These feelings were exacerbated by the hatred of his brothers. We, too, resort to donning masks of bravado, airs of superiority, and even anger to hide our feelings of inferiority and guilt. Sometimes, the garments/masks we wear become such an essential part of us that we cannot even see how we are dressed as we look into the mirrors of our lives.

Up until now, Joseph may have been somewhat oblivious to his brothers' intense jealousy and hatred. His vision was masked by his own self-importance spawned by his father's undisguised favoritism and embodied in his splendid coat. But now, as he was being cast into the pit, uncovered and unprotected, he couldn't help but finally realize that he would be a sacrifice that was meant to ameliorate the pain that he and his father, Jacob, had caused his brothers.

How appropriate, then, that after selling him to the caravan of merchants headed for Egypt, the brothers took the remnants of Joseph's coat and dipped it into the blood of a goat that they slaughtered before returning it to Jacob as evidence that Joseph had been killed by a wild animal (Genesis 37:31–33). The coat that had been worn by Adam and Eve was now dyed red with sacrificial blood.[29]

Because the Rabbis believed that the blood of a he-goat resembles human blood, it was as if the brothers had not only slaughtered the animal, but killed Joseph as well.[30] How ironic! The coat, which symbolized authority and power, was stained scarlet, indeed the color of royalty, but now with Joseph's blood, the symbol of his death at the hands of his brothers (Genesis 37:32–34).[31] The brothers took out all of their anger and vengeance on Joseph's coat, as if they were killing Joseph himself.

They fell upon him as a pack of hungry animals, tearing the garment off of him. They ripped the garment into small pieces with their spears and daggers to make it appear as if it had been torn apart by a wild beast.[32] Simply put, they were ripping Joseph himself apart. When the brothers showed the coat to Jacob, he exclaimed, "A savage beast devoured him! Joseph was completely torn apart!" (Genesis 37:33). Nothing of his son was left, save the bloodstained, tattered coat. Not even a bone fragment was preserved. As Reuben exclaims, "The boy no longer exists [*einenu*]" (Genesis 37:30).[33]

In Dostoyevsky's *Crime and Punishment*, the bloodstained and tattered clothing of Raskolnikov, like Joseph's coat of many colors, also symbolizes the deep-seated anger and rage that lead him to kill Alyona Ivanovna, a pawnbroker and moneylender. His student coat and his shirt, emblematic of his rebellion, play an important role in abetting his crime, just as the *kutonet passim* became the vehicle for getting rid of Joseph and making his father believe that he was dead. Raskolnikov tears the shirt into pieces of cloth, which he sews into the overcoat to conceal the murder weapon—an axe—and following the murders (he also kills Lizaveta, a secondhand clothes dealer!), he wipes the axe on some laundry, once again connecting the crime, guilt, blood, and clothing. He then worries about the bloodstained clothing and, most ironically, winds up carrying the bloody clothing around with him, just as Joseph's coat would underscore that his "murder" would always be part of his brothers' psyche.[34]

If Joseph's coat masked his insecurities and fragility until it was removed from him, now stained and battered, it served to also mask the brothers' hatred and their horrendous act. It was meant to conceal what they had done and to deceive their father. Yet, in effect, the brothers themselves had been unmasked. Although they removed any traces of their sinful behavior, their actions set in motion the series of events that took place over the ensuing twenty years, culminating in their encounter with Joseph.

Their younger brother became the viceroy of Egypt, and Pharaoh placed him in charge of all the food stores. When the brothers went down to Egypt to procure food during the famine, it was destined that they would meet Joseph. During Joseph's tests of his brothers, they admitted to each other, "Alas, we are being punished on account of our brother [Joseph], because we looked on at his anguish, yet paid no heed…. That is why this distress has come upon us." Reuben added in this regard, "Now comes the reckoning of the blood" (Genesis 42:21–22). The coat ironically led to the unmasking and suffering of his brothers as well as of Joseph.

Each of us, just as the sons of Jacob did, eventually must come to understand that those who possess the magical coat from Eden have to use it with great wisdom if it is to enhance them. With power, authority, and status comes responsibility to others, especially those closest to us.

Ripping Apart the Coat: Destroying Joseph

It took Joseph's brothers some twenty-two years to understand the nature of the divine garment, which represents the number of years that had passed between the events at the pit and their self-revelation in speaking with Joseph. Early on, they recognized neither the purpose the coat truly served nor the essence of Joseph, who wore it. They also did not see how their actions affected their father.

When they came to Jacob with the tattered tunic dripping with blood, they proclaimed to him, "We found this. Recognize, please is this your son's tunic or not?" (Genesis 37:32). They callously waved the garment in their father's face, forcing him to see for himself that Joseph had been dismembered, and the once magnificent coat, now in pieces, was all that was left of him.[35]

In a sense, for both the brothers and their father, the coat was Joseph. The brothers had totally obliterated him, as articulated by Jacob in seeing the coat, "*Tarof, toraf Yosefh*," "Joseph was completely torn apart" (Genesis 37:33). They got rid of all that was uniquely Joseph—his irritating nature; the status given him by his father; his dreams of grandeur, which belittled everyone else in the family; the lineage of his mother, Rachel; and of course, his divine coat.[36]

They indeed had removed every trace of Joseph in their lives with the ultimate act of throwing him into the *bor*, a deep pit or well in the ground. This pit, however, was totally empty; there was nothing in it to sustain him (Genesis 37:24). But the word *bor* is used in the Bible to convey other meanings. For example, when Joseph was placed in prison in Egypt as a result of the seduction by Potiphar's wife, the prison itself is called a *bor*. Symbolically, it is also understood as the netherworld, Sheol, the kingdom of the dead (Genesis 37:35). It was as if his brothers had thrown him into a grave, had buried him deep in the ground, and all that remained was for them to place the large stone over the well/pit to effect his death.

But it wasn't only Joseph whom the brothers killed when they ripped his coat into pieces and cast him into the pit. When Reuben, who had saved Joseph's life by suggesting they throw him into the pit with the intention of retrieving him later (Genesis 37:21–22), saw that Joseph had been sold into slavery, he immediately rent his clothes in mourning (Genesis 37:29). Similarly, upon examining Joseph's coat, Jacob rent his own garments, put on sackcloth, and was thrown into his own pit of inconsolable pain and isolation. He refused to be comforted and proclaimed, "I will go down to Sheol in mourning for my son [Joseph]" (Genesis 37:34–35).

Removing or tearing one's garments is used in many cultures as an outward sign of pain and grief.[37] We see the rending of clothing and the wearing of sackcloth frequently throughout the Bible. Whether it be King David mourning the loss of his sons (2 Samuel 13:30–32, 15:30) or King Ahab of Israel when the prophet Elijah castigated him and prophesized that his progeny would suffer (1 Kings 21:27), the tearing of garments is symbolic of the rending of the person in the face of loss. Even God is portrayed as removing the sackcloth after a person has completed the process of mourning (Psalm 30:12). The Rabbis also decided that on certain occasions of loss, such as the death of a parent, the torn garments may never be mended![38]

The tradition suggests that because Jacob was forced to rend his garments and wear sackcloth due to the actions of Joseph's brothers, all the descendants of his twelve sons would be forced to do the same. The entire people would be made to endure the pain caused by the rending of the garment from the Garden of Eden, and that suffering would be experienced not only under Egyptian servitude, but in succeeding generations as well.[39]

Yet, though torn and tattered, the divine coat, like Joseph himself, would survive and preserve the magical light of redemption that was sewn into it in the Garden following Creation. In a most wonderful way, the Qur'an similarly describes the coat as a source of wisdom and prophetic insight. Jacob is pictured as rubbing his eyes with the coat, after the brothers presented it to him and, as a result, was miraculously able to see that Joseph was alive in Egypt.[40] It was as if, when the brothers asked him, "Recognize [*haker*] please [the coat]" (Genesis 37:32), Jacob was able to see the possibility of repair and healing in his family—that the places of pain and isolation, the *bor*, the pit, and perhaps even Egypt itself, *Mitzrayim, metzarim,* the "narrow places," could be transformed.

Ironically, it is the pit that actually saved his life. The brothers may have stripped him bare, but the pit covered him. The *bor* protected him from further harm; in a sense, it was the place of his salvation!

Perhaps we can learn from this that it is possible to transform our perception of the pit in our life, the place of total isolation and pain, into a *be'er*, a well that ensures life. We, however, must then ask: Can we even dream about a time in our lives when the pain that envelops us will dissipate and we will be free? Can we overcome the fragmentation in our own lives and come to wholeness? Can the tattered fragments ever be stitched together? And furthermore, what makes this transformation possible for those of us who feel completely immersed in a place of pain?

As we struggle with these questions, listen to an extraordinary midrash on the pit and Joseph's return to it years later:[41]

While Joseph was viceroy and the entire family had come down to live in Egypt, Jacob died and Joseph led a caravan back to the land of Canaan to bury him in the Cave of Machpelah. The brothers fulfilled their father's request that he be buried on the land that Abraham had purchased, the place in which Abraham and Sarah, Isaac and Rebecca and Jacob's wife Leah were buried.

After a great and solemn ceremony and a period of mourning, Joseph and the entourage left the Cave of Machpelah, but instead of traveling southward directly back to Egypt, Joseph led the caravan northward toward Dothan and the pit into which he was thrown. He had to return to the place of his suffering and terror.

One can imagine the fear his brothers experienced when they realized that Joseph was leading them from the grave [of their father] to the pit of their past, and what might transpire once they arrived there."[42]

Yet, as Joseph stood over the pit, the site of his pain, out of his mouth came words of blessing: "Blessed be God who permitted a miracle to come to pass for me here."

Perhaps it is possible for us to survive the pit and the narrow places, in which we all have dwelt on occasion. The place of emptiness and hurt can be transformed into a source of healing and growth. The garments that envelop us, that at times are tattered and hang by a thread, can be woven again into the coat of splendor once worn by Adam and Eve and handed down through the generations.

5

TAMAR CONFRONTS JUDAH

Masks Can Reveal
More Than They Conceal about Us

Genesis 38:12–19

When the brothers last saw Joseph as the Ishmaelite caravan headed south toward Egypt, they surely thought that they were finally rid of him and his coat of many colors. Ironically, however, Jacob had given a tattered piece of the divine garment to each of them so they would not forget their long-lost brother and his beloved son. And as fate would have it, twenty years later, they were forced to confront him, covered with the robes of Egyptian royalty that masked his identity. Much transpired over the two decades, not only for Joseph but also for his brothers in Canaan.

Judah's Deception of Tamar

During that time, Judah, the most powerful of Jacob's sons, who could have saved Joseph's life at the pit, distanced himself from the family.[1] He went south to the camp of his friend Hirah, the Adullamite, and soon married the daughter of a Canaanite named Shua. She bore him three sons, Er, Onan, and Shelah, and Judah set out to marry off each of them. Er married a Canaanite woman named Tamar (Genesis 38:1–7), but he died shortly thereafter, and

Judah then gave Tamar to Onan in order to fulfill the obligation of a brother to ensure the continuity of his deceased brother's line, called levirate marriage (Genesis 38:8).[2] But when Onan died as well, Judah believed it was due to Tamar, and he feared for his remaining young son Shelah. So even though he counseled Tamar to return to her father's house until Shelah came of age, he never intended to fulfill his responsibility to her. Shelah would not die like his brothers, even if Judah had to deceive his daughter-in-law and not fulfill his responsibility (Genesis 38:11).

This was not the first time Judah had deceived someone close to him, having played a crucial role in the brothers' tricking Jacob into thinking that Joseph had been killed by a wild animal (Genesis 37:31–34). They brought Joseph's coat covered with the blood of the kid they slaughtered and said to their father, "Recognize please, is this your son's tunic or not?" (Genesis 37:32). The coat would disguise their actions, but it also embodied their sinfulness, and Judah still carried a piece of the coat with him.

But it is clear that Judah convinced himself of the justice of what he had done, because he gave very little thought to Tamar from that day forward. He really believed that his treatment of Tamar was justified because he felt that he had saved Shelah's life. Knowing ourselves, we realize just how easy self-deception can be when we can rationalize our behavior. Dare we think of the times we have told untruths or have not fulfilled promises we made in the name of something more important, perhaps knowing that we've done something wrong? In most cases, these involve minor issues, and we label them "excuses" or "stories." We believe that we would never hurt anyone, and we wear this false self-perception as a mask that camouflages the hurt we have caused. Yet, let us learn from Judah's case, because as a result of deceiving Tamar, he lost something of himself.[3]

Ironically, a short time later, Judah's own wife died. Like Tamar, he suffered a terrible loss, though unlike his daughter-in-law who had to wait for Shelah to marry her (the levirate relationship prohibited her from ever marrying another man), Judah could get on with his life.[4] Judah went through a period of mourning and then went up to Timnah with his friend Hirah to join in the sheepshearing festival (Genesis 38:12).

The Uncovering on the Road to Timnah

Judah joined the men in Timnah in order to console himself following his wife's death.[5] He would surely have the opportunity in Timnah to sow his wild oats once again. The symbolism of the sheepshearing is quite clear: the women at Timnah, like the sheep, would be uncovered, and Judah would comfort himself by having a good time during his stay.[6] But perhaps at Timnah, Judah himself would be uncovered, the mask of respectability removed so that he would have to face his true self.

Hearing that Judah was coming to Timnah, Tamar became infuriated. Judah had the power and the prerogative to do whatever he chose after his wife died, but her situation was irreparable. After waiting for years for Judah to act, she realized that Judah was never going to fulfill his obligation of having Shelah marry her. As a result, Tamar was bent on revealing just who her father-in-law was, and in the process, he would really see her for the first time.

As difficult as it must have been for her, Tamar took the initiative and seized the opportunity. She removed her widow's garb, covered her face with a veil, wrapped herself up (*hitalaf*) and situated herself at the entrance (*petach*, which also means "opening" in Hebrew) to a village called Einayim (Genesis 38:14). Even though Tamar may have been terrified to remove her clothes of mourning, don a veil and colorful garments, and sit alone at the crossroads waiting for Judah, she wrapped herself in courage and strength (*hitafal*, reversing the letters of *hitalaf*), fortifying herself for what had to be done. She had changed (*hithalaf*, further playing on the same verb): she was no longer the young, naïve girl at the mercy of her father-in-law, but rather a strong young woman who had the ability to assert herself.[7]

According to the tradition, Petach Einayim was itself synonymous with the crossroads,[8] a place where several roads converged and travelers had to make choices about the direction they would take. Tamar had reached a crossroads, which now would determine the direction of her life as well as that of Judah.

Petach Einayim was located on the road to Timnah (Genesis 38:14), and this was the place where the prostitutes gathered. How powerful, though, that the place's name was Einayim, which means "eyes" in Hebrew.[9] She was situated at *petach einayim*, "the opening of the eyes"! The place's name only served to underscore the disguise that Tamar used to reveal her situation and redress it.

The use of disguise is prominent in many literary works and frequently serves the key purpose of moving the story line toward specific goals. In the case of Shakespeare's *King Lear*, two characters change their apparel. Edgar takes on the appearance of mad Tom in beggarly garb in order to survive his father's attempt to kill him, while Kent appears as Caius to enable him to convey the blunt truth to the king. In both cases, their disguises also take on a form of protest. Edgar's Tom challenges the aristocracy, while Kent's Caius, a commoner, challenges the falseness of the king, Lear, even as he protests against the notion that one must be a member of the court to be of service to the king. Simply put, Caius and Tom, in their poor man's attire, symbolize the "naked" truth.

As a result, they help Lear, like Judah, both remove the mask of royalty and uncover his own false life. Wishing to emulate the basic truth embodied in Tom, King Lear finally removes his own clothes. Ironically, Edgar needs a mask to reveal Lear's false life. Undressed, Lear is like poor Tom—a free man, unencumbered by the superficiality of the aristocracy and the royal court.[10]

Similarly, it would take Tamar, in the guise of a prostitute on the road to Timnah, to open the eyes of her father-in-law to the truth about himself. In masking herself, she intended to unmask Judah, to remove the superficial cover to his true identity.

Judah certainly wore the mask of honesty and sincerity when he instructed Tamar to wait patiently for Shelah to reach maturity so that he could marry her. Neither Judah nor we as readers could have imagined what the upshot of his actions would be; we could not have conceived that Tamar, a simple Canaanite woman, could find a way to unmask her seemingly powerful father-in-law. She, too, would appear "other," but in her case, in the name of what was right and just.

Frequently in literature, we find that clothing is utilized to blur the distinction between appearance and reality. In *Hamlet*, the ghost warns Hamlet that a man may "smile and smile, and be a villain" (1.5.108), and throughout the play, clothing creates as well as reveals the surface world of illusion. Yes, dear Polonius, "the apparel oft proclaims the man" (1.3.72), revealing the discrepancy between the characters' inner and outer lives. Hamlet, for example, makes himself appear disheveled to convince Ophelia that he has lost his mind. He also knows that the clothes of mourning worn by his mother, recently widowed, were merely for appearance's sake, because she marries his uncle a short time afterward. In contrast, his own "inky cloak" sets him apart from everyone else, just as his grief makes him feel like an outsider in the joyful court.

His black clothing literally and figuratively symbolize his presence as death.[11]

Appearance and reality were surely blurred as Tamar positioned herself at the crossroads near Petach Einayim, waiting for Judah to come by. One tradition says that Tamar covered her face and her entire body, and only her eyes were exposed. She, indeed, underwent a radical physical change, and Judah could never have recognized his daughter-in-law, even during sexual intimacy.[12]

Some sources say that Tamar painted her face in dazzling colors,[13] while others contrastingly indicate that she was covered in a white bridal dress, perhaps symbolizing the purity of her intentions, in contrast to her father-in-law.[14] Thomas Mann creatively suggests that Tamar was covered in a *kutonet paspasim*, a striped or tattered garment, which was reminiscent of Joseph's coat.[15] As he approached, perhaps Judah couldn't help thinking that the garment looked like the *kutonet passim*, a piece of which he always carried with him, as he bore the burden of what he and his brothers had done, how he himself had not fulfilled his responsibility.

There are many occasions in the Bible in which characters disguise themselves and appear totally different. This usually occurs to facilitate some purpose that seems justified. When an Israelite prophet confronted King Ahab on the road, he disguised himself as a bondman by covering his face so he could gain access to the king (1 Kings 20:38). The change of garment was meant to enable him to speak God's words of castigation to the king.

Yet, not every change of garment is done for noble purposes. King Saul, for example, disguised himself when he went to inquire of the witch of En-dor about the outcome of his impending battle with the Philistines (1 Samuel 28:7–8). He did not trust in God's power, and therefore in divesting himself of his royal garments, he forfeited his power and authority.[16] Similarly, when the same Ahab, the king of Israel, went to battle against Ben-hadad and the Aramaens, he disguised himself as a common soldier. However, he died in battle because of a lack of courage and faith (1 Kings 22:30).

Just consider for a moment how even we occasionally may disguise ourselves in order to appear "other" than what we really are. How facile are we in donning masks of caring, sincerity, presence, and even love when we perhaps know in the deepest recesses of our conscience that they are somewhat studied and purposeful? And in the end, will we, like Saul and Ahab, suffer because of our actions?

Uncovering of Self and the Other

As he approached, all Judah saw was a Canaanite harlot sitting by the way (Genesis 38:15). He couldn't see that it was his daughter-in-law because her face was hidden. Truth be told, he would not have recognized Tamar even if her face were uncovered. All the time she lived in her father-in-law's house, she covered her face out of her deep modesty, chastity, and respect. He had never really seen her.[17] In actuality, however, he paid no attention to her anyway, never really coming to know her as a person. He saw nothing, even though she spent time in his presence.

But knowing ourselves, how can we be critical of Judah? Have we not fallen prey to the very syndrome, sometimes being with other people, but never really seeing them or hearing them? And this even pertains to those whom we presume to love. We convince ourselves that we are spending quality time with someone close to us, building relationship, getting to know each other, but we really are thousands of miles away, immersed in our own thoughts and selves, oblivious to the other. Truly seeing another person takes work and commitment on our part, a conscious attempt to really pay attention to what is important.

And our ability to recognize the essential makeup of others is exacerbated when they are wearing a superficial covering that camouflages their true self. Like Judah, who only recognized the garments of a prostitute sitting by the wayside, we are taken by the masks that people wear—external trappings that seem to define them: their success, wealth, looks, and friends.

But in contrast, Tamar saw Judah and knew the truth. She understood that he had no intention of ever allowing Shelah to marry her and that she was destined to sit as a widow for the rest of her life (Genesis 38:14). With the passage of so much time, she came to know who he really was in his essence. Sitting at the crossroads at Petach Einayim, she couldn't help ruminating about her years of loneliness, holding on to the hope that one day she would marry Shelah. But now all that was gone. The illusion had to be undone; the mask that Judah had worn publicly all these years had to be removed. In removing her widow's clothing and covering herself, she prepared to expose her father-in-law for what he was. His eyes—and those of all who knew and respected him—would be opened at Petach Einayim. She lifted her eyes (*einayim*) to the gate (*petach*) of heaven, and according to the Rabbinic tradition, prayed to God, "May it be Your will that I not leave this place alone, with nothing."[18] According to the Rabbis, God's eyes watched over all who passed through Petach Einayim, and it was a destination for pilgrims.[19]

Fulfilling the Pledge

Judah, seeing only a harlot and not knowing that the woman sitting on the side of the road was his daughter-in-law, turned aside and told her he wanted to sleep with her. When she responded by asking how much he was willing to pay, he promised to send her a young kid from his flock when he returned home. (Ironically, it was the blood of a kid that covered Joseph's coat when the brothers fooled their father, Jacob. Then, too, Judah failed to live up to his responsibility.) Tamar, however, demanded a pledge, an *eiravon*. When Judah asked about the *eiravon*, Tamar demanded nothing less than his seal (*chotem*), the cord or sash he placed around himself (*petil*), and his staff (*mateh*) (Genesis 38:16–18), the essential symbols of his status, power, and tribal standing. Judah's seal or signet ring bore the image of a lion's head, the very symbol of who he was and eventually of his tribe (Genesis 49:9), the design of his sash was symbolic of his status and that of his family, and his staff was given to him by his father and, handed down over the generations, would become the very staff of Moses![20] But the tradition goes further, stressing that the three items pointed to Israel's future: the signet ring would be used by Israel's kings, a cord of blue was part of the garments of the judges in the Sanhedrin, the High Court, and the staff alluded to the Messiah, whose "mighty scepter will stretch forth from Zion" (Psalm 110:12).[21]

Judah didn't understand (see!) that she was truly entitled to his family status in the first place. Simply put, Tamar demanded his identity, his self. The pledge, the *eiravon*, from the word *areiv*, meaning also "surety" or "guarantee," represented the value replacement of the missing object. In this case it ostensibly was the kid Judah promised to send, but in effect it was Judah's family status to which she was never given access. The pledge here is powerfully similar to the symbolism of Joseph's coat for the brothers and Jacob, because it was all that was left of Joseph.[22]

Although previously unwilling to have her become part of his family's identity, Judah, overcome by passion, agreed to her demand, and in sleeping with Tamar, he unknowingly fulfilled his obligation as a father as well as his implicit pledge (*eiravon*) to her. Unbeknownst to him, Tamar conceived twins as a result of the encounter on the road to Timnah, thereby enabling Judah to provide his two deceased sons with heirs. Tamar would teach Judah that the lost brother must be redeemed, something he had not understood as he stood over Joseph in the pit.[23]

The notion that it was Judah's identity, his family line, that Tamar desired is further underscored by several commentaries and midrashim that understand the *petil* to be a sash or an even larger article of clothing, rather than a cord. It is based on the fact that *petil* frequently means "a thread" in Hebrew and the verb *patal* signifies "to weave."[24] The interpretations vary as to what type of garment is meant, though most Rabbis call it a *simlah*, a kind of decorative tunic or cloak.[25] Others see it as a small cloth wound around one's neck and head in the fashion of a turban, which is a sign of distinction, even of royalty.[26]

There are some interpretations that even go so far as to identify the items that Tamar demanded of Judah with the three things a husband is obligated to provide his wife, among them, her clothing.[27] In our story, Tamar seduced Judah into taking Shelah's place, and she conceived in the process, thus enabling Judah to fulfill the levirate obligation. When she later gave birth to twins, Perez and Zerah (Genesis 38:27–30), Tamar in effect replaced the two lost sons of Judah. It was as if Judah and Tamar were linked as husband and wife, each unknowingly making the other whole again. In addition, because Judah, along with his brothers, had taken Joseph's coat, dipped it in blood, and presented it to their father, thus ignoring his responsibility to Jacob and Joseph, he now was forced to give Tamar his own mantle. Perhaps he had even sewn the tattered patch from Joseph's coat that was in his possession into the garment that he gave to her.

Recognizing Oneself through the Other

Three months later, it became obvious to all that Tamar was pregnant. Judah, hearing that this was the result of her prostituting herself, in his self-righteousness, ordered that she be killed. As she was about to die, she informed Judah, saying, "I am with child by the man who owns these [objects]." Then she added, "Recognize please, to whom do this seal, mantle, and staff belong?" (Genesis 38:25).

As Judah listened to her words, his mind flashed back to the words he had spoken to his own father when the brothers showed Jacob Joseph's tattered coat covered with the blood of the kid: "Recognize please, is this your son's tunic or not?" (Genesis 37:32). The words sounded strangely the same: *Haker na ... ha-chotemet* (Recognize please ... the seal) and *Haker na ha-ketonet* (Recognize please ... the coat), as if one was retribution for the other. Judah's actions vis-à-vis Joseph led directly now to the loss of all that defined him.

Judah was forced to recognize the injustice of his actions—all of his actions, starting with the sale of his brother, and then the deep pain he had caused Jacob and Tamar. As he stared at the seal, mantle, and staff, the most important symbols of who he was—or at least ought to have been—perhaps for the very first time in his life he took a real look at himself. Finally, finally, *vayakeir Yehudah*, "Judah recognized" (Genesis 38:26). What in fact did Judah recognize, see? It was not simply the seal, mantle, and staff, though most biblical translations read: "Judah recognized *them*."[28] What he was able now to see clearly was himself, including the shadow, his other side, that he had never confronted. And as he did, he blurted out for all to hear, "[Tamar] is more righteous than I, inasmuch as I did not give my son Shelah to her" (Genesis 38:26).

This was the turning point for Judah. He took the first step toward essential personal change and greater wholeness in his life. His relationship with his Canaanite daughter-in-law led him back to his brothers, his family, and his higher self. To achieve that, he had to give his own mantle (and his seal and staff), the symbols of his power and all that previously defined him, to Tamar, and in return, the line of kingship, the Davidic line, would be traced through him. One of the twins to whom Tamar gave birth was Perez, who was the first person mentioned in the Davidic genealogy (Ruth 4:18–22).[29]

The irony, of course, is that Tamar's deception led to an essential change in Judah and his life and, as a result, had an ultimate impact on the people of Israel as a whole. Sometimes deception, if justified in some way, can indeed lead to an outcome that is positive and even transforming.

Covering Oneself with Righteousness

The Rabbis say that occasionally a person appears handsome or beautiful, but his or her clothes are unbecoming. It also is possible that people are not very attractive physically, but their clothes are beautiful and well-suited for them.[30] Judah was a powerful, imposing figure, but so much in him heretofore was lacking. Yet, he finally acted justly in his life, donning a garment of righteousness. It was such righteousness that eventually would lead to the messianic age.

The prophet Isaiah portrays both God and the Messiah wearing justice, righteousness, and faithfulness, which will lead to ultimate redemption (Isaiah 11:5, 59:17). But most interesting, some commentaries assert that it is the righteousness of human beings that gird God's strength.[31] Job describes his righteousness in a similar way: "I clothed myself in righteousness and it robed me; justice was my cloak and turban" (Job 29:14). What is also interesting in this regard is that the priestly garments are described as garments of righteousness as well, and their purpose was to help those who sin change their natures and fulfill themselves.[32] This will lead to the redemption of all the righteous. The psalmist writes in this regard, "Your priests, O Lord God, are clothed in triumph, Your righteous ones shall rejoice in [Your] goodness" (2 Chronicles 6:41).[33]

Years after being in large part responsible for the sale of Joseph and causing irreparable pain to their father, Jacob, Judah had indeed changed. And we as readers must be unafraid to ask ourselves if we believe that we, too, have the power to change. Do we have the capacity to see ourselves honestly, as Judah came to recognize himself? Will people eventually be able to say about us, "*Vayakeir*," that we indeed recognize who we are and understand how we might become better?

Judah had changed, but Joseph's coat remained torn and bloodstained, and Joseph was a distant memory, one of the faded lights in the night sky, the very lights that Joseph once claimed would bow down to him. What would become of Joseph? What would become of Judah and his family? Would we ever again see Joseph's coat, the garment that had been handed down through the generations?

6

JOSEPH AND POTIPHAR'S WIFE

Uncovering True Identity

Genesis 39:11–18

When last we heard about Joseph's coat, the brothers had presented it to their father to prove that Joseph had been killed by a wild animal. The coat, dripping with blood, had been torn apart, and Jacob was convinced, as were the brothers, that Joseph would never be seen again. Sold to a band of Ishmaelite traders headed for Egypt for twenty pieces of silver, Joseph in turn was sold as a slave to Potiphar, the Pharaoh's chief steward (Genesis 37:28, 37:33–36). Though each brother was given a piece of what remained of the coat by their father, little did they realize that Joseph was also left with a part of the garment, which he wore as he was carried down to Egypt.

It did not take long for Potiphar to be impressed by Joseph's ability, and he placed him in charge of his entire household. God saw to it that Joseph succeeded in all that he did for Potiphar, and as a result, his master placed everything that he owned in Joseph's capable hands (Genesis 39:1–6). With all of his success, Joseph had little inkling that he was about to be devoured by another "wild beast" and his coat would once again be the pivotal object in the story.[1] As we have already seen, clothing frequently is the vehicle to move the plot forward, sometimes in unanticipated ways.

The Seduction

His meteoric rise in Potiphar's house placed Joseph in a position of power. How far he had come from the pit and his brothers' treatment of him! According to one tradition, Joseph's ego grew as a result of his master's confidence and because the members of the household reacted to him and his appearance so favorably (Genesis 39:6).[2] In his vanity, he began to preen and pamper himself, daubing his eyes and smoothing back his hair. The Rabbis likened him to a man sitting in the marketplace primping himself, in effect saying, "I am quite the man."[3] His beauty was not lost on Potiphar's wife, Zuleika,[4] and she began to cast her eyes on him (Genesis 39:7).[5]

Day after day she wore her finest clothes, bedecked herself in jewels, and beautified herself to catch his attention. The midrash says that she used to change her clothes three times a day; the clothes she wore in the morning she did not wear in the afternoon, and again she put on new clothing at night. Zuleika was very calculating in her attempt to attract the attention of her handsome young slave.[6] She made sure her perfume permeated the house, and she sat in the vestibule through which Joseph constantly passed.[7] She continually tried to coax Joseph into lying with her, but to no avail.

One day, when no one was in the house, she surprised Joseph by grabbing hold of his coat from behind,[8] insisting that he sleep with her (Genesis 39:11–12). As he fled, the coat ripped and he left her holding it in her hand (Genesis 39:12).[9] How powerful is the symbol of her holding the coat in her hand (*yad* in Hebrew), and the text emphasizes it by repeating that Zuleika saw (and understood the implication of) the garment in her hand (Genesis 39:13). Because the hand represents power, it underscores that Potiphar's wife thought she had power over him, but she was left with nothing but a piece of cloth (just as the brothers were left with nothing but his tattered coat). Every time she tried to seduce him, Joseph reminded her over and over again that her husband had placed all that he owns "in my hand," in a sense giving him the power even over her. He went even further by emphasizing that he could never commit such a wicked act and thus sin against God, who is all-powerful (Genesis 39:8–9). The repetition and echoes of the word *yad* (hand) in the narrative highlight the shift from trust to conjugal betrayal,[10] from powerlessness to power.

The language of the text here also betrays Zuleika's intent. It says literally that "she grabbed hold of him [*titpesheihu*] by his garment" (Genesis 39:12), rather than the expected, "she grabbed hold of his garment." It was all about her desire for Joseph, and the coat was merely a symbol of him, representing his special nature and unique beauty. In her eyes, she knew that he placed a large stake in how he dressed and preened himself, and so the coat also manifested his greatest weakness.[11]

According to one aspect of the Rabbinic tradition, it was indeed not easy for Joseph to withstand Mrs. Potiphar's pressure. Not only did he fear the consequences of rejecting the advances of his master's wife, but also his adolescent vanity could easily have pushed him to give in to her seductions. The Rabbis wonder how it was possible for Zuleika to remove his *beged*, his outer garment covering his entire body, without his complicity. Surely it was not simply that Zuleika was able to rip the entire garment off of Joseph in one motion! Thus, doubts are raised in the tradition concerning Joseph's actions in the seduction. When the text says that Zuleika "grabbed hold of him by his garment [*bigdo*]" (Genesis 39;12), some commentators actually suggest that the word also means "his betrayal," from the Hebrew root *bagad*. The choice of the word *beged*, as opposed to a word such as *simlah*, leads some to say that she "grabbed hold of his 'faithlessness.'" He not only had something to do with stirring up Zuleika's passions by his constant primping, but also on that fateful day he entered Potiphar's house not simply to "do his work" (Genesis 39:11), but to "get on with business."[12] The Rabbis noted, therefore, that a person is truly symbolized by his clothing.[13] Zuleika wanted him at all cost and wanted to reduce him to a mere object.[14]

Yet, even recognizing how difficult it must have been for Joseph to reject her advances, in the end Joseph would not be seduced into sinning. He maintained his honor and fulfilled his responsibility in the process. He literally fled (*va-yanos*) from Zuleika and ran (*va-yeitzei*) outside (Genesis 39:12). One verb would have sufficed here, but the doubling—"he fled and ran"— shows that he ran away as fast as he could;[15] the Rabbis described him as "leaping" away from her.[16]

They also suggested that what strengthened his refusal to be seduced was the fact that at the very moment Zuleika grabbed him, he saw his father Jacob's image. It reminded him of the values he had been bequeathed, and this cooled his blood.[17]

An alternate midrashic tradition is that the garment itself protected him. When Zuleika grabbed him, the four corners of his garment, its ritual fringes (the *tzitzit*), slapped his face to awaken him to the reality that his whole future and that of Jacob's progeny were on the line, and he simply could not give in to his masculine feelings.[18] The garment carried with it a vision of what the world should be, a vision of the perfection flowing from Eden, and a hope for the future.

Sometimes, when we as individuals find ourselves in positions of power and authority, it is relatively easy to be seduced by the belief that we can get away with almost anything. Power creates the illusion of being impervious to the consequences of any impropriety; we believe that we will never be discovered.

But what mitigates against our falling prey to these very thoughts? What might we envision in those situations that would prevent us from abusing our power to do as we like, even if it involves hurting others? Do we, like Joseph, carry with us images that can sustain us? What values from our upbringing and experiences fortify us and impel us to reach toward our highest self?

Joseph's upbringing not only led him to reject Zuleika's advances, but some traditions even note that he treated her with respect. As he rushed away from her, he reached back to grab his coat, which she was holding. But in that instant he realized that he would have to wrestle it away from her, which not only would take time, but he also did not want to demean her. She was, after all, Potiphar's wife.[19]

Joseph's Coat Redux

As Joseph was running from the house, the memory of his brothers tearing off the multicolored coat that their father had given him flashed before his eyes. It seemed like almost yesterday, though much time had passed, and he once again experienced the vulnerability that he had felt when he was thrown into the pit.

Seeing the garment in her hand, Potiphar's wife felt that she had the power; as his mistress, she held Joseph's fate in her hands, just as his brothers did twenty years before.[20] She screamed out to the servants and showed them Joseph's coat, claiming that he came to defile her (Genesis 39:13–18). The garment he wore, the very garment that had been handed down over the generations, would once again be a sign of a lie that would determine his future. His brothers used the garment as evidence to convince Jacob he was dead, and he wound up not only in the *bor*, the pit into which he was tossed, but also sold into slavery in Egypt. Also called a *bor*, Egypt was another place of isolation. Now he would be thrown into prison by Potiphar, which powerfully was referred to as a *bor* as well (Genesis 40:15).

To show that Joseph was to blame, she placed the coat next to her, as if Joseph had abandoned it (Genesis 39:15–18). Had she kept it in her hand, it would have seemed like she had ripped the coat off of him. Three times she says that "he left his coat next to me [*etzli*]," as if to stress that he was the guilty party.[21]

But the fact that she kept it near for a time also leads the tradition to say that it was as a substitute for Joseph, the object of her desires. She embraced, caressed, kissed, and fondled the coat as if it were Joseph.[22] She held the garment, still warm with his body heat, as if she held him, capturing his beauty and sensuality.

Perhaps at some time we ourselves have been taken in by the superficial qualities of another person, the individual's physical appearance, his or her sense of power and authority, or maybe the person's wealth. Perhaps we, like Zuleika, were entranced by the person's dress, makeup, or carriage. It is easy sometimes to allow surface characteristics to draw our attention and disarm us. But let us beware of what, perhaps, lies underneath.

However, overwhelmed with feelings of rejection, Zuleika then tore at Joseph's garment, just as his brothers tore the coat in a rage of jealousy years before.[23] She devoured it like the wild beast that the brothers claimed shredded the coat of many colors.

The Coat: A New Beginning

But this time it was different for Joseph. The coat that indeed was the concrete sign of the brothers' deception and Zuleika's false claims now symbolized Joseph's honesty and integrity.[24] In midrashic and Islamic tradition, the fact that the coat was torn from behind was thought to be clear evidence that Zuleika had initiated the contact and Joseph was innocent.[25] In ripping off his coat, the brothers had unmasked him: they had shown just how ridiculous were his dreams and his illusions of self-importance. Of course, it also signaled the violence perpetrated against him, similar to the experience at the hands of Potiphar's wife.[26] Yet, now, as he spurned the advances of his master's wife, he no longer needed a façade to cover his true nature.[27] For all of its importance, Joseph nevertheless left (*azav*) the coat behind, abandoning this material object and saving his soul in the process.[28] Four times in the short scene, Joseph is pictured as "leaving behind," "abandoning" the precious coat (Genesis 39:12, 13, 15, and 18), in a sense casting aside the superficial identity associated with the coat. For the first time, he was able to see the difference between the superficial and the real, and this enabled him to take control of his emotions and his life.[29] The spoiled younger brother was disappearing, replaced by a more mature, responsible adult whose ego needs did not have to be massaged.

It is not at all easy to overcome, let alone let go of, aspects of ourselves that may be deeply engrained. The coat had defined Joseph and how he related to his entire family; it eventually led to his downfall. But even in the wake of the violence done to him by his brothers and its consequences, Joseph held on to the coat, and it continued to adorn him. The way he preened and carried himself in Potiphar's house made it clear that the old, self-consumed Joseph was still somewhat oblivious to his true self. Yet, the confrontation with Zuleika seemed to enable him to begin to see what was truly important and how his life needed to embody a sense of higher purpose.

In Shakespeare's *Measure for Measure*, the removal of clothing also involves unmasking the individual and uncovering the true person. For Shakespeare, as we have already seen, clothing can be a symbol of pretense, which must be removed in order to recognize the essential person. In this play, the Duke dresses as a friar, but wearing the robe borrowed from Friar Thomas and acting like a friar does not make him one. When Lucio pulls back the Duke's hood, uncovering his face, thus revealing his real self, in so doing, Lucio uncovers his own pretense of being a close friend of the Duke. When Angelo removes Mariana's veil, thinking he will uncover a plot, he not only reveals who she really is but also unmasks himself and his own devious behavior in the process. Isabella wisely points out to Angelo that the clothing and trappings of power are insignificant; what matters is the virtue and grace of the person: "No ceremony that to great ones longs, not the king's crown, nor the deputed sword, the marshal's truncheon, nor the judge's robe, become them with one half so good a grace as mercy does" (act 2, scene 2).[30]

Similarly, when Potiphar's wife ripped off Joseph's coat, she revealed the true essential character of her slave, which finally came through. Now Joseph was able to recognize the core of his being. In so doing, Zuleika also uncovered who she was, as well as her lies and deceit.

Joseph's struggle to abandon certain traits challenges each one of us as readers to think about our own particular internal battle with the parts of ourselves of which we are not proud. It is difficult to overcome things that are so ingrained in us and in our way of relating to others. Can we, like Joseph, begin to see some of our less desirable qualities in a different light and then let them go, as he let go of the coat that seemed to be a natural part of him and fit him so well?

From the Pit to Power

Even though Joseph's motivations were pure, Joseph was cast back into the pit from which he was delivered to Egypt and Potiphar's house. Hearing the accusations of his wife, Potiphar became furious with Joseph and placed him in prison with others confined by the king. Hardly had he attained his position of power with Potiphar that Joseph was again stripped of his cloak of authority and position and forced to descend even further into the depths of abandonment. From being his father's favorite to being enslaved in Egypt, he now wore prison garb in the king's dungeon.[31]

All the time Joseph spent in prison, he had dreams of the pit into which his brothers had cast him and even referred to his dungeon cell as "a pit" (*bor*). He pleaded with the king's chief cupbearer, who also was thrown into prison, to mention him to Pharaoh upon the cupbearer's release. In so doing, Joseph said in a most telling manner, "I was kidnapped from the land of the Hebrews; nor have I done anything here that they should have put me in a pit [*bor*]" (Genesis 40:14–15). Joseph's three years in prison ironically paralleled the three days he languished in the pit in Dothan.

During his three-year confinement, Joseph continued to mature, and we encounter a more empathetic Joseph. The once egocentric dreamer was now able to truly listen to others and interpret their dreams, all the while acknowledging God's Presence and help. Not only did he interpret the dreams of his fellow prisoners, but he was also called upon to interpret Pharaoh's dreams. The haughty dreamer had become a vehicle of interpretation, God's voice.[32] As a result, Pharaoh had him taken out of "the pit," had Joseph's hair cut and his clothes changed (Genesis 41:14), and appointed him as viceroy of Egypt. This was the beginning of Joseph's meteoric rise to power. Joseph was given charge of all Egypt in Pharaoh's stead, symbolized by the royal garments of fine linen and the gold chain around his neck, placed upon him by Pharaoh himself. Pharaoh also removed his signet ring and placed it on Joseph's hand, thus symbolizing a transfer of power (Genesis 41:41–42).

According to the Rabbinic tradition, Joseph was finally rewarded for his refusal to give in to Zuleika's seduction. It was understood as measure for measure: because Joseph governed his passions and did not touch Potiphar's wife, he was made the governor of Egypt; because he did not hearken to her words, all of Egypt hearkened to him; because Zuleika caught Joseph by his garment and he left it in her hand, so Pharaoh took off his signet ring and placed it on Joseph's hand; because he had not bowed his neck to commit a sin, therefore Pharaoh put a gold chain on his neck; and because his body had not cleaved to sin, so Pharaoh bedecked him in garments of fine linen.[33]

Covering with a Garment: A Sign of God's Covenant

Covering an individual with special garments, especially those of royalty, indicates a change in status, as was the case with Joseph. This is evident in many passages in the Bible and is particularly poignant when two parties enter into marriage. In these instances, the key phrase used is *lifros kanaf*, "to spread one's skirt or robe" over another. The word *kanaf* usually means "wing," which implies that the man extends his protection over the woman.[34] For example, when Ruth requested that Boaz cover her with his garment, she used these very words, which is seen as proof that Ruth wanted to marry Boaz (Ruth 3:9), just as birds spread their wings over the other when they mate. Commentators also cite Arabic custom as further evidence that when a man places a garment over a woman, it is a symbol of their union.[35]

Just prior to Ruth's clear proposal of marriage, she joined Boaz on the threshing floor, and as the text states, she "uncovered his feet" (va-tegal margelotav) (Ruth 3:7), from the Hebrew word regel (foot). Yet, this rare form of the word for feet (margelot) raises other possible interpretations. Because the similar word margaliyot means "pearls" or "jewels," the verse could mean that Ruth euphemistically uncovered Boaz's genitals. The Rabbis then go on to suggest that what Ruth really uncovered was the core of Boaz's being, who he truly was, as evidenced in his supportive and loving reaction to her.[36]

This custom is also found in the Bible referring to the relationship between God and Israel. Israel's status is changed when God spreads the divine garment over her and she becomes God's covenanted partner. The primary example of this is found in Ezekiel 16, which is interpreted by the Rabbis as referring to Israel's subjugation in Egypt and subsequent liberation.[37]

Ezekiel first portrays Israel in her youth as being utterly sinful by describing her as "naked and bare" (Ezekiel 16:22).[38] This same expression is used in part in describing Adam and Eve in the Garden of Eden following their sin (Genesis 3:10–11). The Rabbinic tradition emphasizes that Israel was not simply unclothed, but she was naked and bare of God's commandments and, therefore, was left totally vulberable.[39] Israel's sole protection was the commandments, which are an embodiment of the covenant with the Divine.

Therefore, seeing Israel's potential, God adorned her with the protective garments of God's covenant. Just listen to a portion of the text:

> So I spread My robe [*efros kenafi*] over you and covered your nakedness, and I entered into a covenant with you by oath—declares the Lord God; thus you became Mine.... I clothed you with embroidered garments, and gave you sandals of dolphin leather to wear, and wound fine linen about you, and dressed you in silks. I decked you out in finery and put bracelets on your arms and a chain around your neck.... Your apparel was of fine linen, silk and embroidery.
>
> (Ezekiel 16:8–13)[40]

Understood metaphorically, God covered Israel with the commandments, thus bringing her into the covenant and ensuring her survival. It is most fascinating that the term *kanaf* also means "corner" and is used to refer to the four-cornered garment worn by some Jews, which represents a reminder of God's commandments, as well as the corners of one's garments on which are attached the fringes, the *tzitzit*.[41]

Contrastingly, when Israel sins, the term *efros kanaf*, spreading one's garment over a prospective bride, is turned on its head to indicate an illicit act. For example, when a man wants to marry his father's former wife, and thereby embarrass him, he would be guilty of "uncovering the corner his father's robe [*kanaf*]" (Deuteronomy 23:1).

According to the same passage in Ezekiel, when Israel once again strays, falling prey and offering herself to foreign gods, she will be left as before—naked and bare. Stripped of her clothing as a sign of her treachery and sinfulness, she will be punished for rejecting God's commandments (Ezekiel 16:35–39).[42] This is most poignantly applied by the Rabbis to the building of the Golden Calf soon after Israel received God's commandments on Mount Sinai (Exodus 33:6). Because of her sin, Israel is metaphorically stripped of her royal garments and ornaments, her status thereby diminished in God's eyes.[43]

The Merit of Joseph and Israel's Survival

Understanding the adorning of Joseph with royal garments as a reward for his rejection of Zuleika's advances, the Rabbis also emphasized that his actions would have long-term consequences for his descendants. Just as Joseph benefited from the merit of those who came before him, having seen his father's image at the moment when he was accosted by Potiphar's wife, so years later the Israelites were rewarded because Joseph fled (va-yanos) Zuleika's grasp (Genesis 39:12). Because Joseph had the strength to flee from Potiphar's wife, when the Israelites approached the Red Sea, the sea fled (va-yanos) from before them (Psalm 114:3). According to the Rabbinic tradition, they survived because they were carrying Joseph's bones with them back to Canaan.[44] Similarly, in Hebrew the splitting of the Red Sea is keriat yam suf; the word kara literally means "tear" or "rip." Therefore, we can opine that it was due to Zuleika's grabbing Joseph's garment and ripping it off of him against his will that the sea parted.

When the Israelites left Egypt, they followed Joseph's instructions and placed his bones (atzmot Yosef) in a casket (Genesis 50:25; Exodus 13:19) and carried his remains with them.[45] Yet, according to the Rabbis, they not only transported his bones back to Canaan, but they also carried his essence with them. With a slight change in vocalization, the term atzmot Yosef, "the bones of Joseph," can be understood as *atzmut Yosef*, the very substance of Joseph's uniqueness.[46]

What ultimately symbolized his essential nature more than anything else was the remnant of the coat that he had received from Jacob and had worn throughout his years in Egypt. When Joseph died, the remnant of the coat of many colors, which represented both his youthful ego and his maturation that began with the confrontation with Zuleika, was placed in his coffin and accompanied him back to his ancestral homeland. What remained of the coat worn by Joseph as well as the additional pieces originally given to his brothers and then handed down to their descendants returned to their original home. Worn by Adam and Eve, and later by several of the patriarchs and matriarchs, the coat now was the possession of the people of Israel as they settled in the Land of Israel.

7

AARON'S DEATH AND THE SYMBOLISM OF THE PRIESTLY GARMENTS

Vehicles of Holiness and Transformation

Numbers 20:22–28

Prior to Adam and Eve leaving the Garden, God clothed them in garments of skins to provide them protection outside of Eden (Genesis 3:21). The clothing represented the presence of the Divine that enveloped them, and the garments were then passed down from generation to generation, finally accompanying the people of Israel on its journey through the desert back to the land of their ancestors.

When the people settled in Canaan, they built the Temple in Jerusalem and continued the sacrificial service begun in the desert. According to the Rabbinic tradition, when the High Priest officiated in the Sanctuary,[1] he was dressed in the very garments that covered Adam and Eve. Yet, when Aaron was consecrated as the first High Priest, God commanded Moses to bring Aaron and his sons before the entire community at the entrance to the Tent of Meeting that was set up in the desert and anoint them into the priesthood by placing the special priestly garments upon them (Leviticus 8:13). The Rabbis noted that the same words were used when God dressed Adam and Eve, suggesting that the tunics worn by Aaron and all the High Priests were symbolically if not actually the garments from Eden.[2]

The Power of the Priestly Garments

The priestly garments were considered to be holy, embodying an essence of the Divine.[3] Because the garments themselves possessed sanctity (Ezekiel 42:14), they most certainly could invest all those who merely came into contact with them with holiness (Ezekiel 44:19). The Rabbis went so far as to stress that while the priests were covered in the priestly garments, they were "clothed" in the priesthood, but when they were not wearing the holy garments, the priesthood was not a part of them.[4]

Therefore, it was almost as if God's Presence were evident when one encountered the High Priest clothed in his white garments; surely the *Ruach ha-Kodesh*, God's Holy Spirit, rested upon him.[5] To some, the High Priest was even seen as an angel of God when he performed the sacrificial service.[6] Occasionally in the Bible, the spirit of God is pictured as actually "dressing" a priest, as we see in 2 Chronicles: "Then the spirit of God enveloped Zechariah son of Jehoiada the priest" (24:20).

The importance of white robes in Jewish ritual persists to this day, while it also appears in other religions. Even the Catholic pope is distinguished by his everyday white cassock or robe. The *kittel*, Yiddish for "robe" or "coat," from the German, meaning "house/work coat," is worn not only by rabbis but also by traditional Jews. It serves as a burial shroud, but it is also worn on special liturgical occasions by Ashkenazic Jews. In Western Europe this garment is called a *sargenes*, related to the Old French *serge* and the Latin *serica*. Some Orthodox Jews wear a *kittel* when leading a Passover Seder, and the cantor wears it during special prayer services, such as the penitential prayers (*Selichot*) prior to Rosh ha-Shanah, the seventh day of Sukkot, and the first day of Passover, on which the prayers for rain and dew are recited. In many traditions, the bridegroom wears a *kittel* on his wedding day.

Like the High Priests of old, married men traditionally wear a *kittel* on Yom Kippur, though in some communities it is also worn on Rosh ha-Shanah. The use of the *kittel* on the High Holy Days is usually linked in the Rabbinic tradition to the forgiveness of sins, based on the relevant verse in Isaiah, "Be your sins are like crimson, they can turn snow-white; be they red as dyed wool, they can become like fleece" (Isaiah 1:18). In addition, the wearing of the *kittel* reminds the individual on Yom Kippur of his or her eventual death (because it is used as a shroud) and instills feelings of humility, brokenheartedness, and remorse, which should lead to repentance and symbolic rebirth by the end of the day.

The white color of the *kittel* more generally symbolizes purity, innocence, light, and life. The use of colors plays an important role in all literature, representing a character's qualities, emotional moods, and hierarchical position. The colors white and red are especially powerful and prevalent.

In Tennessee Williams's *A Streetcar Named Desire*,[7] written in 1947, the symbolic meaning of Blanche's name, which in French means "white," is a signature of the play. When she first appears, she is dressed in a white suit, white gloves, and a hat. The color white stands not only for purity and innocence but also for perfection and virginity. But Williams is the master of irony here, because the color stands in complete contrast to Blanche's behavior. Blanche is a highly promiscuous seductress. As a result, later in the play she is pictured as wearing a scarlet satin robe, the reddish color symbolizing love, passion, and fertility, but also blood and fire. Contrastingly, Stanley wears colors exactly the opposite of Blanche. He and his friends dress in blues and sometimes greens. The first time their garments are mentioned, they are wearing blue denim work clothes. Blue is a symbol of strength, calm, authority, and truth.[8]

The color red is used at various times in the Bible to represent sinfulness and punishment. A classic example occurs in Isaiah in which God is described punishing the sinners: "Why is your clothing so red, your garments like his who tread grapes? I trod out a vintage alone.… I trod them down in My anger, trampled them in My rage; their life-blood spattered My garments, and all My clothing was stained" (63:2–3). The prophet describes God destroying the nations who are sinful, and their blood, their life-force, is splattered all over the garments of the Divine. Although God is pictured as initially only wanting to tread upon them like grapes and extract their wine, God eventually destroys them.[9] Similarly, red is the color of the Avenger: his garments are red, his warriors are red, and their shields are red (Nahum 2:4).

The sense of the almost godlike nature of the High Priest is most evident in the rapturous portrait of the High Priest serving in the Temple on Yom Kippur, the Day of Atonement. Based on material in the Wisdom of Ben Sira,[10] the following part of the Yom Kippur liturgy is known as the *Avodah*, the Temple service. Imbibe the power and beauty of these words from the traditional liturgy:

> *In truth how glorious was the High Priest*
> *as he came forth from the Holy of Holies*
> *in perfect peace.*
> *As the brightness of the vaulted canopy*
> *of heaven was the countenance of the*
> *priest,*

As lightning flashing from the splendour
of the Chayyot [the winged creatures on
the Ark],
As the celestial blue in the thread of the
ritual fringes,
As the iridescence of the rainbow in storm-
clouds,
As the rose painted in the midst of a pleasant
garden,...
As a diadem set on the brow of the king,
As the mirror of love in the face of the
bridegroom,
As a halo of purity shining forth from the
mitre of holiness,...
As the morning star shining in the borders
of the east,
was the countenance of the priest.[11]

This is similar to Ben Sira's description of Simon, the son of Yohanan, the High Priest, as he donned his glorious robes and clothed himself in perfect splendor.[12] It is the clothing more than anything that impelled the people to sense God's Presence.

As was mentioned, the Rabbinic tradition stresses that these garments invested the priests with God's holiness, sanctifying them as they entered the priesthood. Listen to the words of the paradigmatic biblical text from the book of Exodus: "You shall instruct all who are skillful ... to make Aaron's vestments for consecrating him [*lekadesho*] to serve Me as priest" (Exodus 28:3).[13] The garments themselves were suffused with holiness (*kodesh*), and they transferred their sacredness to the individuals who wore them.

Yet, these external garments are also understood as symbolizing the inner qualities of those who wore them; in a sense, they were "vestments of the soul." This clothing was not fashioned by the artisans, but rather by Moses, who was to instruct the priests in the improvement and embellishment of their souls and characters. It was their inner selves that had to be clothed in majesty and splendor.[14]

Similarly, in *The Canterbury Tales*, Chaucer uses the garments and accoutrement of the different characters to define their core natures. They symbolize what lies beneath the surface of each personality. The reader cannot help but know that the Physician loved wealth, because he is described as wearing a gown of rich silk and fur. The Squire's youthful vanity is underscored by the excessive floral brocade on his tunic, and the Merchant's forked beard points to his essential duplicity.[15]

As we reflect upon the fact that the priestly garments necessarily pointed to the requisite deeper inner qualities of those privileged to wear them, we cannot help but think about how we occasionally get caught up in superficiality, neglecting matters of deeper meaning. We who are in positions of authority, for example, perhaps put too much stake in the external trappings of our status, forgetting that passionate devotion to our responsibilities and caring about those whom we serve and with whom we work are the true measures of our success.

It is also noteworthy that the priests dressed in their splendid garments were compared in the Rabbinic tradition to the kings of old bedecked in their royal clothing, as well as to a bridegroom wearing his white wedding *kittel*.[16] Perhaps the vestments of the High Priest, which carried the aura of the garments placed on Adam in the Garden of Eden, symbolized the covenant between God and Israel and therefore the expectations of both the priest and those whom he served.

In this regard, the Rabbis suggested that just as the sacrificial offerings enabled Israel to atone for its sins, so, too, the garments worn by the priests were instruments that led to atonement.[17] This tradition is extended to suggest that each one of the eight priestly garments, the four outer garments worn by the High Priest and the four inner garments that all priests wore, atoned for a specific category of sins. In addition, they were worn in a very strategic manner, placed on the High Priest's body in areas that signified the nature of the sin for which the garments atoned: the ephod, the vest, for idolatry; the trousers for sexual transgressions; the *kutonet*, the tunic, which covers most of the priest's body, for bloodshed; the breastplate for corrupt judgment; the cloak for evil gossip; the crown for haughtiness and arrogance; the headband for effrontery; and the belt, wound around the body and worn over the heart, for improper thoughts.[18]

The clothes that the High Priest wore enabled him to transcend his own individual human needs and take on a more universal import. Through his garments, he was able to reach out to others and make atonement for all humanity.

Depending on the particular activity with which the priests were engaged in the Temple, they were instructed to wear specific garments that befit each role. As a result, they were constantly putting on (*lavash*) and taking off (*pashat*) different articles of clothing.[19] When they entered the Tent of Meeting, they removed their linen garments, stored them away, and dressed in more appropriate clothing for their sacrificial tasks.[20] The holiness of the garments had to be preserved, and the Rabbis offered a simple analogy: a person should not offer a cup of wine to his teacher while wearing the garment in which he has just finished cooking for him.[21]

Of course, when the priests left the sanctuary, they removed the garments in which they fulfilled their functions, leaving them in the outer vestibule. It was forbidden to mix their holy garments with those of the people outside, because the object was to maintain a distinction between them and the nonpriestly Israelites. Therefore, the Israelites were even forbidden to touch the priests' vestments, as the priests themselves were prohibited from touching the garments of the people.[22]

Perhaps the challenge for many of us today in positions of authority is how we wear the symbolic garments that mark our roles, status, or level of achievement without isolating ourselves from others. We occasionally struggle to find a suitable balance in our lives between the person who we are on the outside, in our careers, and the individual without the suit and tie, without the uniform. And then we have to ask whether we, unlike the priests of old, have the capacity to draw close to other human beings, realizing that one significant aspect of our happiness is dependent on the relationships we establish with those in our closest circles of friends and family.

The Garments Make the Priest

The importance of the priestly garments and their symbolic power is no more evident than in the scene of Aaron's death in Numbers 20. At Mount Hor, God commanded Moses to take Aaron and his son Eleazar up to the top of the mountain and strip Aaron of his High Priest vestments and put them on his son. Moses did as God commanded. They ascended Mount Hor, and Moses stripped Aaron of his garments and placed them on his brother's son. Aaron then died on the mountain's summit (Numbers 20:23–28).[23]

Aaron's existence, indeed his entire identity, was defined by his role as High Priest. So when Moses stripped him of his garments, it was tantamount to stripping away all of who he was.

It involved a total uncovering. This is underscored by the fact that the description of Moses undressing Aaron interestingly includes two separate elements: Aaron and his clothes. It is as if the biblical writer were stressing that he stripped Aaron as well as his clothing. In removing his brother's priestly vestments, Moses in effect was stripping away the very core of his brother's being.[24]

When Aaron was consecrated as the High Priest, he underwent a total transformation that effectively gave him a new identity. Now, at the moment of his death, he was stripped of who he had been these many years. The Rabbis took note of the fact that the very language used in the Bible when Aaron was inducted as the High Priest—"Take Aaron," *Kakh et Aharon* (Leviticus 8:2)— was repeated here when the symbols of his role were removed (Numbers 20:25).[25] The vestments of the High Priesthood radically changed him and served as symbols for who he was.

So, should we ask ourselves whether the garments we have donned in our careers have changed us in essential ways, and if so, has this always been for the good? Have the roles we assumed become so much a part of us that they have carried over to all aspects of our lives and served to define us? Perhaps once this happens, it is very difficult to symbolically remove the garments, in effect unmasking ourselves and revealing our true personae.

Moses removed the garments he had given Aaron when he consecrated his brother as High Priest, the clothing that defined Aaron's nature for almost four decades. God, at the same time, took back his soul, his divine essence.[26] Listen to the fanciful midrashic rendering of the conversation between the two brothers on Mount Hor as Moses tried to inform Aaron of his impending death.

> Moses said, "Aaron, my brother, has God given you anything in your keeping?" "Yes," Aaron replied. "What

was it?" asked Moses. Aaron said, "He has placed in my charge the altar and the table upon which is the show-bread." Moses said, "It may be that God will now demand back from you all that He has given into your keeping." Aaron asked, "What, pray?" Moses replied, "Has He not entrusted a light unto you?" Aaron responded, "Not one light but the seven of the menorah [candelabrum] that now burns in the Sanctuary." Moses had intended to call Aaron's attention to his soul, "the light of the Lord," which God had given into his keeping and which now He demanded in return![27]

At the very moment that Aaron was stripped of his priestly vestments, he also lost the light that enveloped him in the Sanctuary, which had protected him. It was the very light with which God had covered Adam and Eve and that they carried with them out of the Garden.

It was quite evident to the Rabbis that as long as Aaron was clothed in his priestly garments, he was protected from all harm, including the Angel of Death. The garments prevented the priests from bearing any of the iniquity of the people's sins as they sought atonement for them (Exodus 28:43).[28] This was especially true of the frontlet, the *tzitz*, made of pure gold, upon which was engraved the inscription "Holy to Adonai," which could never be removed from Aaron's forehead (Exodus 28:36–38). As long as Aaron wore the priestly vestments, he was immune from all evil. Even death could not touch him.[29] Yet, the moment that the garments of light were removed, Aaron became vulnerable and immediately died. The removal of the garments was tantamount to the loss of the person he had become—the High Priest of Israel.[30]

Lest we think that having been stripped of the garments of the High Priesthood Aaron was now left totally naked, lacking any identity, the tradition stresses that he still had on the four basic garments that every priest wore. Although he could no longer serve the Divine as the High Priest in the Sanctuary, his basic identity as a priest was preserved. Even in death, his status as a Kohein, one of priestly lineage, was to be recognized by all Israel.[31]

The moment that the High Priest's vestments were stripped from Aaron and he was about to die, Moses immediately placed shrouds upon him, further enveloping him as he journeyed into the afterlife.[32] Although he had lost his essential identity as High Priest, his dignity and humanity were nevertheless protected. Some sources even suggest that it was God, the Divine Self, who covered Aaron in the shrouds, thus giving him even greater honor in his death than during his lifetime.[33]

Continuity and Change: Eleazar Becomes the High Priest

As Moses removed the High Priest's garments from Aaron prior to his death, he simultaneously placed them on Aaron's son, Eleazar. As he removed each garment, Moses tried to comfort Aaron by telling him how blessed he was. Lamenting that his own sons were not involved in the life of the people and would not follow in his footsteps, he told Aaron of the glory of having his son assume his role as High Priest, thereby ensuring that Aaron's legacy would be perpetuated.[34] Moses could not bequeath his crown of leadership to his children, but Aaron should be greatly comforted to witness his son assuming his role and donning the very garments he had worn for much of his life.[35]

Eleazar inherited the position of the High Priesthood from his father as Aaron's vestments were placed upon him. At that moment, he was enveloped by the divine glory, as were those in previous generations who had worn the garments from Eden. The symbolic crown of the High Priesthood was his, yet in his wearing it, he stood in a chain of tradition that reached back to Adam and Eve, the last link in the chain being his own father. Aaron's legacy was preserved, his immortality ensured.[36]

As Moses saw Aaron handing over his core identity to his son Eleazar and realized the loss he himself felt in not being able to transfer his values, worldview, and commitments to his own two sons, we, too, are confronted with our relationships with our children. We, too, need to ask to what extent our sons and daughters have embraced in their own lives that which is meaningful to us. How many of us, like Moses, struggle with the fact that our children have not resonated with our own life commitments, have even rejected the core values of our lives? Those of us whose whole lives are driven by a deep commitment to Judaism must ask whether we have succeeded in transferring that devotion to the next generation.

It is difficult to imagine how Aaron must have felt as he watched Moses take off his garments and place them on his son. As each of the vestments was placed upon Eleazar, Aaron's sense of pride, gratitude, and blessing must have increased tremendously, especially when he saw Eleazar kiss the High Priest garments.[37] His life surely seemed to have felt whole as he witnessed with his own eyes his son being served by Moses, just as he was, and showing Eleazar the honor and respect that was once due him.[38] There was a good reason why the tradition emphasized that even a son of a High Priest, when appointed to take his father's place, was required to be consecrated when he assumed office—perhaps not only to differentiate him from his father, seeing his potential holiness in its own right, but also to enable his father to witness firsthand his own legacy and realize that after he died, his essence was alive in his son.[39]

Let us not ignore the fact that Aaron was wearing the High Priest's vestments on Mount Hor; generally, these garments could only be worn at the time of his service in the Sanctuary. Nevertheless, he climbed the mountain with Eleazar and Moses bedecked in the special garments, and consequently, they were transferred to Eleazar before his father died. The Rabbis suggested that the exception of allowing him to wear the garments outside the Sanctuary was made to emphasize that Eleazar deserved to be appointed to take his father's place.[40]

The Transition between Aaron and Eleazar

At the climactic moment on Mount Hor, Moses followed God's directive and stripped Aaron of his garments and placed them on Eleazar. Because of the holiness of each of the High Priest's vestments and because of the honor due both Aaron and Eleazar, the Rabbis were concerned with the order in which Moses removed Aaron's garments as he placed them on Eleazer.

It was assumed that Moses did not remove all of the garments from Aaron and then place them all on Eleazar. How could Aaron be left standing there bereft of his holy garments? Rather, the Rabbis pictured Moses taking off one garment at a time and then sequentially placing each garment on Aaron's son.[41] However, this presented an impossible problem: if Moses removed the garments from Aaron starting with the outer garments, how could he dress Eleazar in the proper order?

In this moment of transition, according to the tradition, a great miracle happened. The Rabbis creatively suggested several possible miraculous alternatives. One suggestion was that Moses was able to remove the garments closest to Aaron's body first so they could be placed on his son.[42] Aaron was thus able to see that each and every garment found its rightful place prior to his death. He was comforted by the sight of his son, Eleazar, wearing each garment he had worn throughout the years of his service.[43]

Another midrashic tradition says that as Moses removed Aaron's garments, God made sure that celestial garments appeared underneath. It was as if the *Shekhinah* itself enveloped Aaron with divine clothing that took the place of the priestly vestments.[44] It seemed to Aaron that the very *ananei kavod*, the Clouds of Glory, that accompanied the entire people on its journey through the desert toward the Promised Land now would accompany him on his journey to the next world.[45] Therefore, before he was buried, Aaron was arrayed in eight divine garments prior to being covered with the shrouds.[46]

Another possibility put forth was that as Moses removed Aaron's garments one by one, the angels were present and placed each of them on Eleazar in order. It was as if God were dressing Aaron's son and protecting him, as the Divine had protected his father.[47]

One final fantastic suggestion as to how Moses removed Aaron's garments in order without leaving Aaron naked of all of his priestly clothing while he dressed Eleazar was that the mountain itself covered Aaron. As Moses removed each garment from Aaron, the mountain swallowed the part of his brother's body that was exposed. When all the garments were removed, it was as if Aaron were already fully buried on Mount Hor, and no one would ever know where he was buried.[48]

How powerfully similar this was to Moses's death when he ascended Mount Nebo, facing the Land of Israel. He also seemed to simply disappear, with no one knowing the site of his burial place (Deuteronomy 34:5–6). For all intents and purposes he, too, was swallowed up by the mountain, never to be seen again.

The Impact of Aaron's Death

When Aaron died on Mount Hor, Israel mourned for him for the requisite thirty days (Numbers 20:29), just as they would following Moses's death (Deuteronomy 34:8). Israel was immediately aware that Aaron had died, not only because Moses and Eleazar descended without him, but also because the Clouds of Glory suddenly disappeared. Not only did the people see (*va-yiru*) that Aaron was gone (Numbers 20:29), but also, playing on the verb in Hebrew, they feared (*va-yiyru*) the loss of their protection. The very divine garments that had enveloped Aaron as his High Priest's garments were removed and that now covered him in death no longer protected Israel.[49] They were now exposed for what they were, uncovered and bereft of all that had hidden their sins.[50] The Rabbis noted that Israel was like a woman whose hair was uncovered because of her sinfulness.[51]

Israel was now vulnerable in God's eyes, because Aaron's death involved the removal of the garments of the High Priesthood. Yet, the Rabbis believed that the death of the righteous was also a vehicle for atonement. Aaron, who had sought atonement for Israel through the sacrifices he offered, now atoned for Israel's sins even as he died.[52]

Nevertheless, the divine garments that Aaron had worn now adorned his son Eleazar and would continue to ensure Israel's position as God's covenanted partner. To remind Eleazar of his ongoing obligation to the people as High Priest, as it was his father's, the two stones attached to the shoulder pieces of the ephod had the names of the twelve tribes of Israel engraved upon them (Exodus 28:6–12). All that he would be as High Priest was intended either to respond to the needs of the people of Israel or to atone for their sins. This was the raison d'être of his position—ensuring Israel's survival.

Thus, the garments of Eden, representing the light of perfection and the promise of return to the Garden, would continue to link Israel to its past, guarantee its survival as it entered the land promised to their ancestors, and point to its future as well as that of all humankind. The garments would be handed down through the generations of judges and prophets, kings, and other leaders.

8

DAVID DONS SAUL'S ARMOR

Wearing Our Own Garments, Embracing Our Own Identity

1 and 2 Samuel

The garments of Eden were symbols of Israel's survival, and once the people had settled in their land, they were worn not only by the priests but also by Israel's prophets and kings. Two key early personalities were the prophet Samuel and Israel's first king, Saul, whom Samuel had anointed. However, Samuel soon became disenchanted with Saul when he did not obey God's command to annihilate the Amalekites because of their attack on the Israelites on their journey from Egypt (1 Samuel 15). Samuel informed Saul that God therefore had rejected him and that he, Samuel, would not remain with him. As the prophet turned to leave, somehow a garment was torn in the process (1 Samuel 15:26–27).

Unfortunately, the biblical text is not clear who grabbed whose garment, because the verse literally reads, "*He* grasped the edge of *his* garment and it tore" (1 Samuel 15:27).[1] There are other places in the Bible where a similar lack of clarity exists. When, for example, King Jeroboam of Judah was challenged by the prophet Ahijah, the text says, "*He* had put on a new garment ... and Ahijah took hold of the new garment *he* was wearing and tore it into twelve pieces (1 Kings 11:29–30). Such unclear texts lead to a variety of interpretations on the part of biblical commentators and the midrash alike.

Rending the Fabric of Saul's Kingship

The most prevalent Rabbinic interpretation of what transpired is that King Saul grabbed the edge or corner of Samuel's robe, inadvertently tearing it. Knowing that he had sinned and incurred God's wrath, Saul wished to remain in Samuel's good graces. To prevent Samuel from abandoning him, and wishing to accompany him to the sanctuary at Gilgal,[2] Saul reached out and desperately held on to the prophet's robe.

According to this reading of the text, Saul clutched at Samuel's garment in the hope of retaining his relationship with the prophet and, through it, his kingship and recognition by God. By grabbing hold of the corner (*kenaf*) of Samuel's garment, the king indicated his submission to the prophet and to God's authority. In several cultures, grabbing the hem or corner of a garment signifies political submission.[3]

We noted previously that the spreading of a person's garment or perhaps even the corner of the garment (*lifros kenaf*) over another symbolized the affirmation of the relationship or covenant.[4] The antithesis of this—the breaking of the relationship—would then be symbolized by the tearing of (the corner of) one's garment, *likhrot kanaf*.

If a person's garment is symbolic of the identity and the status of that person, then Saul's grasping at the corner of Samuel's robe is indicative of Saul's desire to maintain his covenant with God and thus his kingship at all cost (1 Samuel 15:35). The irony, of course, is that the robe tears, predicting the complete rupture of their relationship and the ripping apart of Saul's monarchy.

Is Saul's desperate grasp of Samuel's robe so alien to our own experiences? As we encounter Saul's response to Samuel, his hope of repairing his relationship with the prophet and maintaining the status quo, perhaps it recalls how we have acted in the past. Have we, in our desperation, tried to hold on to relationships following our own indiscretions or inability to live up to expectations? Like Saul facing the possibility of never seeing Samuel again, did we then grasp at any straws to simply "hold on"? And when we have vainly attempted to repair our relationships, did it not occasionally make matters worse?

Yet another Rabbinic interpretation understands the tearing of the garment in a different way, suggesting that it was Samuel who grabbed hold of Saul's robe and intentionally tore it.[5] Samuel then said, "Adonai has this day torn the kingship over Israel away from you and has given it to another who is worthier than you" (1 Samuel 15:28). Samuel's actions not only foretold the rending of Saul's kingship but also intimated that the person who would tear Saul's garment in the future would succeed him as the king of Israel.[6] Thus, when David later tore the corner of Saul's garment, Saul said to him, "Now I know that you shall surely reign and that the kingship over Israel will remain in your hands" (1 Samuel 24:21).

Saul, now utterly horrified at the sight of his torn garment and realizing its implications, pleaded with Samuel, "I did wrong, but please honor me in the presence of the elders … and in the presence of Israel, and come back with me" (1 Samuel 15:30). Saul felt rejected, abandoned, and alone and reached out for some comfort and assurance.

Some of us who have served in positions of authority and leadership can resonate with the pain that Saul must have felt as he witnessed his power, authority, and status being symbolically torn away from him. Even if we, like Saul, could have admitted that we were at fault and the decision to remove us from our position was justified, we, too, might also simply have done whatever we could to continue in our role. And we, too, would have been concerned about how our peers would see us and how they would react to our demotion.

But if Samuel's intention was to tear Saul's garment, the biblical text should have read, "Samuel seized the corner of Saul's garment and tore it [*va-yikra'eiyhu*]," instead of saying that it was inadvertently torn.[7] The nearly identical wording is found in the case mentioned before when Ahijah prophesied that Jeroboam would succeed Solomon as king of Israel. Ahijah grabbed hold of his new robe and rent it (*va-yikra'eha*) into twelve pieces (corresponding to the twelve tribes), announcing that God would tear asunder Solomon's kingdom and deliver ten of the pieces into Jeroboam's hands (1 Kings 11:29–31). The rending of the garments in both cases was a clear prediction of what was to come. In the case of Ahijah and Jeroboam, it appears that the prophet tore his own garment, as opposed to Jeroboam's robe.[8]

Some Rabbis also suggested that in our passage Samuel grabbed his own garment and tore it as a result of his regret in having anointed Saul as king in the first place. The biblical writer might have underscored this by saying, "Samuel grieved over Saul, because Adonai regretted that Saul was made king over Israel" (1 Samuel 15:35) immediately after the Bible stated that "the corner of the garment was torn" (27). The midrash emphasizes in several places that the righteous have a tendency to tear their own garments when their plans and vision do not turn out well.[9] This certainly applies to any schism that involved the Davidic monarchy.[10]

Similarly, when Moses sent the spies to scout out the land of Canaan prior to the Israelites crossing the Jordan, ten of the twelve returned with a report that it would be impossible for the Israelites to defeat the powerful inhabitants. Upon hearing their view, the other two spies, Joshua and Caleb, who believed that they could defeat their enemies, tore their garments (Numbers 14:6). The rending of their clothes demonstrated that they rejected the words of the majority of spies and were disgusted by them. The schism among the spies was concretized by the tearing.[11]

David and Goliath: Donning and Removing Saul's Armor

As the Israelites prepared to engage the Philistines in battle, Goliath, the Philistine champion, stepped forward and challenged them to send out a man to fight him. David, who was a mere lad and had only come to the battlefield to check on his brothers, volunteered to take on the giant from Gath (1 Samuel 17:1–37). Saul clothed David in his own armor, placing a helmet and breastplate on him and girding him with his sword. As the king, Saul had the strongest suit of armor of any of the Israelites. However, as one could imagine, under the weight of the armor, David was unable to walk, let alone fight. He tried vainly but simply could not and had to remove the king's armor (1 Samuel 17:38–39).

Scholars who study the nature of clothing and appearance vis-à-vis a person's identity speak of both role embracement and role distance. Role embracement refers to a close link between a particular role and the individual's identity. The role is likely to be integrated into one's self-concept. On the other hand, role distance relates to a lack of inner identification with a particular role. Often, in both these instances, how the person feels wearing particular clothing that signifies the role is crucial. This is especially the case in contexts that are novel to the person, when new and different garments are worn. In these cases, self-awareness is usually heightened.[12] The case of David attempting to wear Saul's armor makes these concepts very clear.

Saul's armor, in Hebrew called *madim*, was custom made for him, and he was head and shoulders taller than anyone in the Israelite camp. The term *mad* (and the more frequent *middah*) means "measure," underscoring that they were tailored to Saul's measurements.[13] *Middah*, however, also means "characteristics" or "qualities," indicating that the garments represented who Saul was, his essential nature. In this interpretive light, David took off the garments, refusing to assume Saul's identity.[14] He had to be his own person if he were to defeat Goliath and ensure the survival of God's covenanted people. This was a clear anticipation that David would eventually replace Saul as king and establish his own monarchy. David simply could not assume Saul's identity.

But many individuals do attempt to embrace the identity and role of others, sometimes to their own detriment. They assume the appearance of others and, in so doing, are essentially changed. Changing clothing can have a drastic affect on individual behavior. Note the classic case of *Macbeth*. Shakespeare utilizes clothing to symbolize not only the change of power in Scotland but also the essential changes in Macbeth himself. As soon as Macbeth is told that he has been made the Thane of Cawdor, he says, "The Thane of Cawdor lives. Why do you dress me in borrowed robes?" (1.3.108–9). Not only does Macbeth not believe that the prediction of the witches has come true, but also, like David, he feels totally uncomfortable in another's clothing, another's identity. Yet, by accepting the new garments and new role, he also loses himself while taking on the Thane of Cawdor's traits. Macbeth's dressing in "borrowed robes" effects his change into a monstrous murderer. The moment he becomes the Thane, he cannot stop contemplating the killing of Duncan so he can become king. His entire being has changed. And after killing Duncan, Macbeth rapidly becomes a control- and power-hungry madman.

Unfortunately, as Shakespeare emphasizes, Macbeth's new title and role never fit him. His title, as Shakespeare says, "hangs loose about him, like a giant's robe upon a dwarfish thief" (5.2.21–22). Macbeth simply does not fit properly into his "borrowed robes." He should have never accepted the title of Thane of Cawder.[15]

In contemplating the implications of David's actions, his rejecting Saul's armor and preferring to face Goliath with merely his slingshot and his shepherd's bag full of stones, can we think of times when we attempted to wear someone else's symbolic garments that simply did not fit us? Sometimes, we might have even tried every which way to make them fit. Did we ever undertake a role or assume a position that did not match who we were? Were we seduced by the beauty or cost of the clothing, or rather, were we insightful enough to realize that the clothes just were not us: they didn't fit our personalities, goals, or values? Did we have any sense of role distance?

However, some Rabbinic traditions fancifully suggest the opposite—that even though Saul was much larger than David, when Saul placed the garments upon David, they miraculously fit him perfectly. From the moment it was predicted that David was to be Saul's successor, the divine spirit enveloped David, and he grew in stature.[16] He was ready to become the king. Some Muslim traditions add that whoever killed Goliath would have a horn placed on his head whose oil would spill over and anoint him at that very moment, and the horn would remain on his head in the shape of a crown.[17] There are indeed occasions when an individual can grow into a role or become comfortable in assuming a new identity.

When Saul realized that his garments somehow actually fit David, making him appear as a bona fide warrior, he was taken aback. His face blanched, and he grew increasingly agitated and angry. In his eyes, it was as if the garments and his kingship were made for David.[18] He was convinced that David would someday replace him.

We can imagine Saul saying to himself, "Who in the world is that little kid taking my place?" In our hearts we know how difficult it is to stand by and witness someone else wearing our clothes, poised to assume the role we have played that heretofore defined us. Even if we realize that nothing lasts forever, it is painful to see our potential successor already acting as though we were gone. If we have been placed in this situation, how did we handle it? Were we any more successful than Saul was in accepting our disappointment?

Yet, David immediately knew that he had raised Saul's envy and perhaps even offended him. As a result, he simply refused to wear the garments that symbolized the kingship.[19] Although he may have hoped that ultimately he would become king, he nevertheless was able to suppress his ego and bide his time.

Wearing Jonathan's Garments: Sharing a Pact of Brotherhood

However Saul saw David and whatever his motivation, he co-opted David into his service, and David soon became very close to the king's son, Jonathan, who loved David. Their deep affection led to a covenantal bond between them, the symbol of which was Jonathan giving David his cloak and tunic along with his armor (1 Samuel 18:1–5). Saul would eventually try to kill David; nevertheless, Saul's son and David created a pact of friendship.[20] Although Saul's armor did not suit him, David proudly wore Jonathan's garments.

The exchange of garments and armor has been used as a symbol of covenant and friendship between apparent combatants in classic literature as well. For example, In *The Iliad*, as the Greeks and Trojans were poised for battle, Diomedes and Glaucus meet in no-man's-land and speak. They eventually decide that they will not fight each other, taking a pledge of friendship. As a sign of their pledge, they exchange their armor.[21]

By transferring of his garments to David, Jonathan indicated that David was worthy of inheriting his father's kingship, though as his father's firstborn, he was the designated heir. The garments fit David, ensuring that he would be successful on all the missions on which Saul sent him, having appointed David as commander of the Israelite army. When he returned from defeating the Philistines, the women came out singing David's praises, chanting, "Saul has slain his thousands; David, his tens of thousands!" Saul was deeply vexed and upset, and he came to fear David (1 Samuel 18:5–15).

Giving David his garments was a sign of loyalty and honor, and from that moment on, Jonathan submitted himself to David's authority.[22] In fact, not only was he David's confidant, sometimes acting against his own father, but he also served as David's second-in-command (1 Samuel 23:15–18).

In giving his garments and armor to David, Jonathan in effect stripped away a part of who he was and gave himself over to David. Clothes unequivocally symbolize who the biblical characters are, so that when they transfer their clothing, the characters in a sense become one.[23]

As we contemplate Jonathan giving his garments to David out of his love for him, it is natural to ask how we might feel sharing our clothes, our identity, with another. Have we ever truly given ourselves over to someone, in effect limiting ourselves in order to establish a relationship? Were we trusting enough to share ourselves, believing that in giving over a part of us, we would actually become more of who we are? Or were we fearful of establishing a deep mutual covenant, never really trusting the other to reciprocate?

Saul Joins the Ecstatic Prophets

As a result of Saul becoming distressed by the women singing David's praises, and realizing that the people envisioned David as the next king, Saul was overtaken by an evil spirit. He began to rave uncontrollably and sought to kill David (1 Samuel 18:8–11). With Jonathan's help, David managed to escape and sought refuge with Samuel and his band of ecstatic prophets in Ramah. Saul was on his way there when the spirit of God caught hold of him and he began to speak as one of the ecstatic prophets (1 Samuel 19:18–23). When he reached Samuel's camp, acting as one of the prophets, he then stripped off his clothes and remained (literally, "he fell," *nafal*) naked all that day and night. The people then asked: "Is Saul now one of the ecstatic prophets?" (1 Samuel 19:24).

As in so many of the biblical narratives we have analyzed thus far, Saul's shedding of garments seems to represent a moment of essential transformation. Similarly, in *Hamlet*, a radical change of clothing represents an essential change in character, though perhaps Hamlet consciously decided to play the role of a madman. Ophelia describes the change in Hamlet: "My lord, as I was sewing in my closet, Lord Hamlet, with his doublet all unbraced; no hat upon his head; his stockings fouled, ungartered, and down to his ankle; pale as his shirt; his knees knocking each other, and with a look so piteous in purport as if he had been loosed out of hell to speak horrors—he comes before me" (2.1.1). If it is assumed that Hamlet makes himself appear disheveled in order to convince Ophelia that he's lost his mind, then we can assume that he is banking on the convention that one's clothing is a reflection of one's state of mind. Based on Ophelia's description—that he is "as pale as his shirt"—Hamlet appears like a ghost of his former self.[24]

If there is a chance that the change in Hamlet was intentional, it seems that was not the case with Saul. By removing his royal garments, Saul gave up his power and authority; in effect, he became naked and bare of all that was the kingship. But there is more. Saul is also portrayed as prophesying and standing naked before Samuel. Because Saul is described as "falling [*nafal*] naked" (1 Samuel 19:24), the Rabbis emphasize that he fell upon his face, prostrate before Samuel, almost as if he had finally submitted to Samuel's authority. The tradition describes Saul here as if he had become one of Samuel's disciples.[25] As Saul lies naked before Samuel, we as readers experience a narrative anticipation of Saul being stripped of his kingship.

The Cutting of Saul's Garment

Saul's moment of transformation did not last very long. When Saul returned from fighting the Philistines, he reverted to pursuing David, as David deftly continued to evade him. Told that David was encamped in the wilderness of Ein-Gedi, Saul took three thousand handpicked men and set out in search of David among the caves inhabited by the wild goats surrounding Ein-Gedi (1 Samuel 24:1–3).

At one point, Saul entered a cave to relieve himself; in Hebrew the idiom is *l'ha-seikh et raglav*, literally, "to pour on his feet," from the root *nasakh*. Unbeknownst to Saul, David and his men were hiding in the back of the cave (1 Samuel 24:4). Yet, just as

David had protected himself by hiding in the cave, so, too, is Saul portrayed in the tradition as seeking cover by entering the cave. Instead of reading the Hebrew verb as "to pour," the Rabbis read it as "to cover," from the root *sakhah*. They even creatively suggested that the cave was like a booth, a *sukkah*, hiding him.[26] However, it was to no avail. Saul had entered the cave so as not to remain vulnerable to attack, yet as it turned out, it seemed that he was about to die.

David's men saw the hand of God in the turn of events. Saul was at David's mercy, and the fulfillment of Samuel's prophecy that the kingship would be taken from Saul was about to come to fruition (1 Samuel 24:4–5).

However, Samuel had actually prophesied that the person who would tear Saul's robe would surely take his throne (1 Samuel 15:27–28).[27] Indeed, instead of killing Saul, David stealthily went and cut off the corner of Saul's garment. As previously pointed out,[28] *kanaf* can mean "corner," and in our passage, David tore or cut (*va-yikhrot*) the corner (*kenaf*) of Saul's robe (1 Samuel 24:5). The verb for cutting is *karat*, which is also used idiomatically when one establishes a covenant—*likhrot berit*. As David ripped the corner of Saul's garment, he, in effect, tore apart Saul's kingship and established his own. He symbolically removed Saul's authority and power, and the covenant Saul had with God as king of Israel.

How amazing! Saul was totally vulnerable and subject to David's power, having been caught in the cave alone and unguarded. David could have done with Saul as he pleased; he surely could have killed his nemesis. Yet, according to one aspect of the tradition, in his heart he knew this was wrong. How could he kill God's anointed ruler! He then prevented his men from attacking the king (1 Samuel 24:6–8). Saul's fate as well as his own was to be left in God's hands, who would judge between them (1 Samuel 24:13–16). He even went so far as to point out to Saul, "See, the corner of your cloak in my hand; [I could have killed you] but I did not" (1 Samuel 24:12). David merely cut the corner of Saul's garment to prove to the king that he had no evil designs on his life. David simply wanted to convince Saul to stop pursuing him.

The entire incident demonstrated David's essential character and courage. He could have killed Saul, who was unrelenting in his pursuit of him, but he somehow was able to curb his baser instincts, his *yetzer ha-ra*. He proclaimed to Saul, "You must plainly see I have done nothing evil or rebellious" (1 Samuel 24:12).

Yet, though he didn't harm the king, David knew that even cutting Saul's garment was a way of disgracing Saul and elevating himself. He thus bemoaned what he had done. Therefore, the Rabbis emphasized that whoever mutilates a person's garment will ultimately have no benefit from it. This would be the case with David and his kingship. When David grew old, we are told: "He was advanced in years, and though they covered him with garments, he never felt warm" (1 Kings 1:1).[29] In the end, the garments of kingship did not make David immune to strife and pain. Although David would replace Saul as the king of Israel, his entire life, especially his family life, would always be tumultuous and unsettled.

Might we ask ourselves whether we have ever been tempted to symbolically cut the garment of someone for whom we worked, someone whose position we coveted? This may have been especially the case if we felt that the individual did not have our best interests at heart. In such a case, what was it that might have tempered our desire to bring down the person and thereby disparage him? Were we, like David, impelled by an inner voice that forced us to understand the root of our feelings and then channel our impulses in a different way? And more, did we have any inkling that we would not benefit from such behavior in the long run?

Upon hearing David's words, Saul broke down and wept, admitting how badly he had treated him and, as a result, how God would reward David (1 Samuel 24:17–19). The Rabbis believed that Saul would have reconciled himself to David had it not been for Abner, a commander in the king's army. Abner constantly provoked Saul, reminding him of David scornfully holding the corner of Saul's royal robe in his hand. Abner chided the king by saying, "What do you care of [David's] pronouncements? The robe was caught in a mere thornbush."[30] According to Abner, Saul's garment could not be damaged by the likes of David, and he egged the king on, urging him to continue to pursue David.

The Rending of the Garments: Acknowledging Saul's and Jonathan's Deaths

Yet, history would take its course. When the Philistines defeated Saul and the Israelite army near Mount Gilboa, both the king and his three sons were killed, including David's beloved Jonathan. A man came from Saul's camp, with his clothes rent and dirt on his head, reporting that Saul and Jonathan were dead. As proof, the messenger brought Saul's crown and presented it to David (2 Samuel 1:1–10). Although the battle between the forces loyal to David and Saul would last for some time, it was at the moment that David was given Saul's crown that the transfer of power symbolically occurred. David would surely become Saul's successor.

Yet, in that moment David couldn't help but mourn the deaths of his king and his best friend. He, too, rent his garments, as did all his men, and he wept and fasted, and uttered a dirge that was recorded for posterity (2 Samuel 1:11–27).[31]

Perhaps we, too, have experienced the loss of our own predecessor, someone who paved the way for us on our career paths. And no matter how close or not we personally felt to that person, we, like David, could focus only on the loss of our superior, perhaps our teacher or our leader. We mourned an individual who had a great impact on our lives. All else may have faded for the moment, and we were left bereft as we also began to contemplate our own eventual demise.

The rending of one's garments was a frequent symbolic gesture in the Bible upon hearing of the death of Israelite leaders, especially in the context of military defeat or even in anticipation of it.[32] For example, King Hezekiah rent his clothes and covered himself in sackcloth as the Assyrians were threatening Judea (2 Kings 19:1–3). Similarly, Jeremiah put on sackcloth when the Babylonians were advancing (Jeremiah 4:8).

Although David's garments were rent in mourning, he nevertheless wore Saul's crown and Jonathan's tunic and armor. David represented the continuity of leadership and the future of his people Israel. David, who was about to become king of Israel, wore the garments passed down over the generations, which would eventually be handed over to the prophets. They, in turn, would transmit God's words, which would guarantee the survival of the people and their covenant with God.

9

ELIJAH AND ELISHA— TRANSFERRING THE PROPHET'S MANTLE

Passing on Authority, Wearing It in Individual Ways

1 and 2 Kings

With the collapse of the Davidic dynasty, the divine garments worn by King David and his successor Solomon were not passed down to the subsequent kings of Samaria and Judah. Rather, they became the possession of Israel's prophets. In the course of time, the most identifiable symbol of the prophet was the garment he wore, and there was none more recognizable than Elijah, the foremost prophet who was the herald of the messianic age.

The Sign of Prophetic Calling

When Elijah confronted the servants of Ahaziah, the king of Samaria, the Northern Kingdom, about the king's idolatrous acts, they reported to Ahaziah that the prophet had predicted his death. The king inquired about this man who claimed the king would die and was told that "it was a hairy man with a garment tied around his waist." The king immediately identified his adversary: "That's

Elijah, the Tishbite!" (2 Kings 1:8). There was no mistaking both Elijah's hairiness and his garment of skin.

It was clear that the prophets wore distinctive garb.[1] This is underscored when a false prophet tried to deceive the people by removing his "prophetic mantle." The only way the masses could initially identify the prophets was when they donned the divine garments from Eden (Zechariah 13:4–5). In the instance of Elijah's confrontation with Ahaziah, the prophet was wearing a sash or belt made of animal skins (in Hebrew, an *eizor 'or*) around his waist.

According to the Rabbinic tradition, Elijah's belt was made of the skins of the ram that Abraham sacrificed in place of Isaac on Mount Moriah. The Rabbis believed that just as the ram saved Isaac's life, so, too, would all of its parts be used to ensure and celebrate the redemption of the Jewish people.[2] The ram, which they suggested was created in the twilight of the sixth day of Creation, just prior to the expulsion of Adam and Eve from the Garden, was seen as a redemptive vehicle, not unlike the very garments that Adam and Eve carried from Eden into the world beyond. The ram and the garments were given to humankind to protect them on their sojourn in this world. And Elijah, the herald of our return to the ultimate Garden, wore a belt made of the skins of that very ram as well as a garment from Eden.

What is fascinating in this biblical scene is that Elijah is described as a hairy man (*ba'al sei'ar*) who was wearing a sash or belt of animal skin. It was as if Elijah were covered by both his long hair and the garments from the Garden. Because we see other references to prophets wearing a "hairy mantle" (*aderet sei'ar*), perhaps a coat made of fur (Zechariah 13:4), it was only a matter of time until later texts conflated the dual description of Elijah and suggested that Elijah himself was the first prophet to wear an *aderet sei'ar*, a hairy mantle.[3] More recently, even Martin Buber pictured him as long-haired, wrapped in a hairy garment with a leather girdle, which was reminiscent of the Babylonian mythic hero Enkidu from the Epic of Gilgamesh.[4]

The pointed description of Elijah as being hairy and wearing a hairy mantle is reminiscent of Esau, who appeared as possessing a "hairy mantle" (Genesis 25:25) and was a "hairy man," in contradistinction to his brother Jacob, who was smooth-skinned (Genesis 27:11). Esau was seen as somewhat wild—a hunter and a man of the fields—unlike Jacob, who was mild and a stay-at-home (Genesis 25:27).

Elijah, too, is characterized by episodes of wild behavior, including his taunting of the priests of Ba'al, shouting and mocking them in a contest with their respective gods (1 Kings 18:25–29), outrunning the chariot of King Ahab (1 Kings 18:46), and being taken up to heaven in a whirlwind (2 Kings 2:11). Ironically, in Hebrew the word for whirlwind/storm is *se'arah* (from *sa'ar*), which is close to the word *sei'ar*, meaning "hair."

Later in the prophet's mission, when he fled to the desert, fearing King Ahab and his wife, Jezebel, Elijah encountered the Divine and immediately wrapped his mantle (*aderet*) about his face (1 Kings 19:13). Elijah did not want to see God's Presence with his own eyes.[5] This is reminiscent of Moses's hiding his face when he encountered God at the Burning Bush. He, too, feared seeing God face-to-face (Exodus 3:6).[6] The tradition goes out of its way to emphasize the many similarities between these two extraordinary prophets, as we shall soon see.

Those of us who grew up in traditional Jewish homes can resonate with the actions of both Elijah and Moses. Being of priestly descent—I am a *Kohein*—I had the extraordinary experience in my youth of participating in the full Priestly Blessing in the holiday liturgy. This was an extraordinary, almost mystical ceremony. It was known as *Duchenen*, because the priests of old stood on a raised platform, a *duchan*, in the Temple in Jerusalem when they blessed the people. I frequently stood next to my grandfather among the other *Kohanim* as we raised our hands, covered our heads with our tallitot (prayer shawls), and intoned the words of Numbers 6:24–26. It was believed that the spirit of the Divine hovered over the priests during this mystical ceremony. As such, the members of the congregation also averted their eyes so as not to see God's Presence. The tallit, like the prophet's mantle, afforded protection from the direct exposure to the Divine.

The Passing of the Mantle

When Elijah encountered the Divine Presence in the desert, he was told by God to go and anoint Elisha, the son of Shaphat, as a prophet in his stead. He found Elisha in a field, plowing with twelve yoked oxen, and threw his mantle over him. Elisha immediately left the oxen and followed after Elijah (1 Kings 19:16–20). The irony is that Elisha, who himself was tied to the yoked oxen that were under his supervision, was now ready to attach himself to Elijah and find shelter under his garment.[7]

This was the moment of Elisha's initiation as Elijah's successor. As we already have seen in the transfer of Aaron's garments to his son Eleazar (Numbers 20:25–28), frequently the inauguration of a successor in the Bible includes the symbolic transfer of the predecessor's garments.[8] In covering Elisha with his mantle, the garment worn by Adam as he left Eden, Elijah passed on his authority and power and the spirit of the Divine to Elisha ben Shaphat. Elisha was now covered not only by Elijah's robe but also by the Divine Presence. This was the moment of his sanctification as a prophet, even though he would not gain actual possession of Elijah's mantle until his master died.

We know well the symbolism of passing a garment from one generation to the next, ensuring a link from past to present, ensuring continuity. This is especially powerful when it involves a moment of dedication and consecration, as is the case with Elisha succeeding his mentor Elijah as God's prophet to Israel.

The wedding custom of wearing "something old, something new, something borrowed, something blue" is a symbol of good luck that goes back to the Victorian era. Something old is meant to represent a link with the bride's family and their past. One extraordinary example occurred recently when a bride named Allison Shellito walked down the aisle wearing a 127-year-old family heirloom. Four generations of brides, spanning three different centuries, were married in the very same wedding gown. The dress was handmade in 1884 for Allison's great-great-grandmother Nelle, who wore it on her wedding day. It wasn't worn again until 1941 by Allison's grandmother. Then her aunt and finally her mother were married in the very same gown. However, Allison insightfully noted, "I think that everybody wore the dress differently; there was something unique about it for each of us. I think it looked different on me than it did on my grandmother, my aunt, or my mom." Now the dress awaits another trip down the aisle.[9]

So, too, would be the case for Elisha ben Shaphat, who would define his own unique role as a prophet. Although he carried on the work of his mentor, Elijah, he surely would place his own stamp on the role.

According to one later Rabbinic tradition, Elijah did not cast his entire mantle over Elisha, but rather brushed him with the corner, the *kenaf*.[10] This may have been a test to see whether Elisha actually was ready to sacrifice his comfortable position and his material wealth to become a prophet. It must have seemed like such an ambiguous gesture that he could have simply ignored it. Yet, he immediately arose to follow Elijah, perhaps realizing the deeper symbolism of being touched or covered by the corner (the *kenaf*) of another's garment, as we saw in the story of Joseph and Zuleika. He was ready to enter into covenant not only with Elijah but with the Divine as well. He was willing to sacrifice the material goods he possessed, concretized by the oxen, and take upon himself the *ol malchut shamayim*, the "yoke of heaven," which symbolized the covenant and its commandments.

Perhaps we have had a similar experience when we were chosen to take over a position of authority, when the mantle was passed to us. Brushed by the possibility of assuming a position to which we never aspired, let alone even considered ourselves capable of fulfilling, how did we react? Did we begin to embrace the possibility that those who thought highly of us saw something in us that warranted their trust and investment? After overcoming our incredulity, did we, like Elisha, have the confidence to leave our place of comfort and set out on a new path, or did we opt to remain in our place of comfort?

The Magical Mantle Divides the Waters

Elisha followed his master everywhere. He did not leave his side, for he knew that Elijah would soon be taken from him by God. Prior to God miraculously taking Elijah up to heaven in the whirlwind, Elijah and Elisha had come to the Jordan River, and the two wanted to cross over. Elijah took his mantle, rolled it up, and struck the water with it, thus dividing it into two parts (2 Kings 2:1–8).

Elijah appears like one of the Greek epic heroes who through the grace of the gods are given magical objects that enable them to succeed. Sometimes this involves magical garments that guarantee the heroes' survival. Such is the case with Odysseus, the hero of Homer's *The Odyssey*, who struggles to overcome myriad obstacles to return home to Ithaca after the Trojan War.

Odysseus is favored by the gods and constantly receives their help, sometimes in the form of magical objects. When, for example, Odysseus's men are turned into swine by Circe, Hermes gives Odysseus a magical herb that prevents Circe from using her spells on him and enables him to free his men. When Poseidon strikes Odysseus's ship with lightning, our hero is able to survive the raging waters because a goddess named Ino had given him a magical cloak. The cloak prevents Odysseus from drowning.[11]

It is also impossible to read this narrative about Elijah and not see the parallelism and resonance with the story of Moses dividing the waters of the Red Sea by extending his rod over the sea. The tradition says that two prophets arose from the tribe of Levi: Moses, the first of all prophets, and Elijah, the prophet who will usher in the messianic age in the time to come.[12] God initially commissioned Moses to go to Egypt and redeem his people, saying to him, "Behold, I will send you [using the verb *shalach*] to Pharaoh" (Exodus 3:10). Moses redeemed the Israelites from Egyptian slavery and ensured their survival by parting the Red Sea with his outstretched arm. Moses was responsible for the paradigmatic redemption of the Jewish people. Similarly, God said, "I will send [*sholeach*] Elijah, the prophet, to you on ... the day of Adonai" (Malachi 3:23). God sent Elijah to bring that initial redemption to fruition in the end of days and ensure that Israel would survive in the here and now by raising up his disciple, Elisha, and demonstrating to him the miracle of parting the waters.

But this midrashic tradition suggests that Moses and Elijah were alike in many respects, not the least of which was that both communicated with God in the wilderness (Exodus 3:1 and 1

Kings 19:4), both were called "man of God" (Deuteronomy 33:1 and 1 Kings 17:18), and God took both at the end of their lives, no one ever being sure what happened to them (Deuteronomy 34:5–6 and 2 Kings 2:11).[13]

Indeed, Moses's use of the rod and Elijah's use of the rolled-up garment symbolize both the presence and the power of the Divine and our ability as God's creations to access that redemptive power. But we, like Elijah, have to be aware of God's power in us and around us, and we have to use that power for the good. We all wear the garments taken from Eden, but they will enhance us only when we invest ourselves in them. The seeming miracle can only occur if we recognize that we are the vehicle to make it happen.

According to one Rabbinic tradition, the waters of the Jordan in the Elijah story were divided into two separate paths, providing Elijah and Elisha each a way to cross the divide. The river was divided due to the merit of both Elijah and his disciple,[14] and these duel paths were also indicative of the ultimate individuality of Elisha. His master would soon die, and he would set out on his own journey to make God's spirit manifest. Although up to this point he was constantly linked with Elijah, the two of them always acting together, Elisha would soon set his own path.

It was at the Jordan River that their paths diverged. Perhaps the division of the Jordan symbolized that master and disciple soon would be separated permanently. At God's behest, Elijah came to the Jordan from Jericho to the west and sought to cross the river, thereby leaving the Land of Israel proper. Crossing over to the other side is clearly a narrative anticipation of Elijah's miraculous departure from this world; he would soon cross the boundary of human existence.[15]

Elisha Dons His Master's Mantle

As Elisha and his master were walking and talking, a fiery chariot and horses appeared, separating Elisha from Elijah, and Elijah ascended to heaven in a whirlwind. When he could no longer see Elijah, Elisha grasped (*va-yachazeik*) his own garments and rent them in two (2 Kings 2:12). Just as Elisha was separated from his master, so, too, were his very garments torn asunder. The tearing of his clothing symbolized his own feeling of being torn apart; he now experienced in essence the loss of a part of his own being, perhaps the part that Elijah had recognized and brought out in him.

Elisha had lost his teacher, his mentor, and he naturally rent his garments in mourning. According to the Rabbinic tradition, just as a person is required to rend his or her garments upon the loss of a parent, so, too, must the individual do so when he or she loses a teacher. Because our text specifically states that he tore his garments into two pieces, the Rabbis go a step further in stressing that they would/should never be completely sewn up again.[16]

Those of us who were fortunate to be particularly close to an individual who played a key role as a mentor can easily understand this moment in Elisha's life. Drawn away from his comfortable life as a successful farmer and having left behind all that identified him in order to follow Elijah, Elisha is now left torn and bereft. We perhaps had those very feelings of loss when someone who changed our lives and provided us with new direction, challenge, and advice was no longer present. Like Elisha's clothing, our own garments may still bear evidence of the rupture we felt.

And like Elisha, we, too, faced the challenge of keeping alive what we received from the one who taught us such valuable lessons and insights, even while we set our own course and vision. It is not easy to differentiate ourselves from a teacher or mentor who had a major impact on us, even as we cherish and hold on to his or her teaching, preserving the mantle.

Immediately, however, Elisha picked up (literally, "he raised up," *va-yarem*) the mantle that was dropped by Elijah (2 Kings 2:13), as though he had bequeathed to his disciple the spirit of prophecy as an inheritance. In raising up his teacher's garment, the very clothing from Eden that Elijah had used to cover his face in God's Presence, the spirit of God was transmitted to Elisha. Elisha, himself, was raised up in the process. The garment, handed down over the centuries, now was the possession of Elisha; he now could act in his teacher's stead.[17]

Following Elijah's death, Elisha would cross the Jordan and return to the Land of Israel to serve God. He took his master's garment and struck the waters of the Jordan while crying out, "Where is Adonai, the God of Elijah?" Although he was a novice in the prophetic role and perhaps doubting his own power, the waters nevertheless parted to the right and to the left, just as they had when Elijah used his mantle to divide them (2 Kings 2:14–15).

But the parallels are even more telling. The Rabbis said that everything done by God, the righteous do as well. In this case, both Elisha and Elijah before him parted the waters, just as God had caused the waters of the Red Sea to part (Exodus 15:8). Not only Elijah, but also Elisha, his disciple, acted with godlike power.[18] If only we could realize the potential we each possess to navigate the bitter waters of our lives, using our garments to make our way through the waters to the Promised Land.

Yet, the Rabbis also argued that the miracle performed by Elisha at the Jordan was twice as great as Elijah's. The initial parting of the waters was due to the merit of both Elisha and Elijah, because both were present and both crossed the river. However, after Elijah departed this world, it was only Elisha's power that caused the Jordan to part a second time.[19] Elisha had internalized the wisdom and experiences of his teacher and now had the ability to cross the Jordan on his own and return to Israel.

Elisha became a prophet in his own right and began his return to the world and to the role that he and Elijah had left together. He assumed Elijah's role in several clear steps: First, he tore and removed his own garments when Elijah disappeared, thus stripping himself totally of his former identity. But, divesting himself of one identity, he then immediately embraced another by donning Elijah's mantle, which had come from Eden. He enveloped himself in the divine spirit that Elijah possessed and that he coveted. Indeed, Elijah's spirit had settled on him, and Elisha wasted no time relying on it (2 Kings 2:15).[20]

Yet, he was to be his own person. Although he called upon the God of Eljiah as he struck the waters of the Jordan, unlike his mentor, he did not roll up his garment. Nevertheless, the biblical text goes out of its way to emphasize that the waters parted to the right and to the left so he could pass through, just as they had when Elijah struck them (2 Kings 2:14). And when Elisha arrived at Jericho, the other prophetic disciples, upon seeing him, bowed low to the ground before him (2 Kings 2:15). Surely Elisha now was blessed with the spirit of the Divine, symbolized by the prophet's mantle that adorned him.

Elijah Ascends to Heaven Covered by the Clouds of Glory

Having raised up a disciple to carry on the work of the Divine in his stead, Elijah was ready to complete his journey to the other side. As with Aaron when he ascended Mount Hor, the garment of Eden was removed from Elijah. Also like Aaron, when his mantle fell from him, Elijah was not left uncovered and vulnerable. He, too, was enveloped by the Clouds of Glory as he ascended to heaven in a whirlwind riding a chariot of fire (2 Kings 2:11–12).[21] The divine spirit still rested upon him, protecting him like shrouds protecting the dead on their journey to the next world.

Elijah could depart this world assured that the mantle he had worn these many years now rested upon the shoulders of one who surely would protect it and ensure its continuity. Like Aaron and all those who preceded him in wearing the garments of light fashioned by God in the Garden, Elijah had passed on the divine garments. They were handed down with the hope that one day they would be worn when Elijah himself would herald the fulfillment of the promise of redemption and the return to Eden.

10

ESTHER, MORDECHAI, AND HAMAN

Change of Garments; Change of Identity
The Book of Esther

The garments first worn by Adam and Eve as they ventured forth into the world outside the Garden of Eden were passed down through the generations. Biblical patriarchs and matriarchs, kings, prophets, and priests, all were adorned with these divine garments, and they served as vehicles of their leadership that ensured the survival of the Jewish people. In addition, the donning of these garments and their removal represented changes in identity and status.

There is no biblical narrative in which the motif of donning and removing clothing is more apparent, powerful, and dramatic than the Scroll of Esther. Set in Persia in perhaps the fifth century BCE, this story of the triumph of Queen Esther, her cousin and foster father Mordechai, and their Jewish brothers and sisters over the evil Haman, who sought their annihilation, moves from scene to scene based upon the change of garments of each of the leading characters.

The Scroll of Esther is all about revealing and concealing. On the deepest theological level, even God is concealed; God's name is never mentioned. Ironically, however, the Rabbis stress that the very name of Esther (*Ester*) reveals God's absence, applying God's own promise to Moses prior to his death, "I will indeed keep my face hidden [*astir*] on that day" (Deuteronomy 31:18). The circumstances alluded to in this verse from Deuteronomy are applied to the days of Esther and Mordechai, perhaps implying God's abandonment of the Jewish people and their eventual destruction.[1] Similarly, much of what is apparent on the surface of the narrative masks a different reality.

Note, in this regard, the character named Elisa Allen in John Steinbeck's *The Chrysanthemums*. She is a lonely, ignored, frustrated farmer's wife with a very mannish physical appearance who, nevertheless, possesses deep, hidden passions. What lies underneath the surface is masked by the clothes she wears: gardening clothing as well as masculine garments. At one point, Steinbeck describes her as wearing "a man's black hat, clod-hopper shoes ... and heavy leather gloves." Although Elisa may be trying to repress her sexuality and conceal her desires beneath these garments, Steinbeck whets the appetite of the reader by intentionally allowing her essential nature to occasionally peek through. For example, though a very feminine print dress is covered almost completely by a large corduroy apron, we get a glimpse of the dress underneath. The manly gloves she wears in the garden protect her hands but also reveal that she wants to be a woman. Unfortunately, when she finally gets in touch with her sexuality and passion, and has what seems like an orgasmic experience, she quickly retreats. She realizes that she will never have it again and symbolically turns up her coat collar so her husband Henry won't see her crying; she withdraws once again into herself, resigned to live an unhappy, isolated life as a planter's spouse.[2]

Although clothing indeed can mask that which lies under the surface, concealing what is essential, it can also reveal the nature and status of those wearing the garments and give us insight into what eventually will happen to them.[3] In seeing how the garments worn by the three principle characters in the Esther story bind them together and what the clothing can tell us about each, perhaps we will be able to uncover larger lessons about ourselves and our own changing circumstances.

Rending One's Garments: Facing Destruction

First, let us recall that the story opens with Esther replacing Vashti as Ahasuerus's queen. At Mordechai's instruction, Esther did not reveal her Jewishness, hiding behind her beauty and her grace (Esther 2). Over time, Mordechai learned of Haman's plot to massacre all the Jews as well as King Ahasuerus's decree that sealed their fate. Mordechai then tore his clothes, put on sackcloth, covered himself in ashes, and sat down in front of the palace gate. The Jews in every province of the kingdom also wept, fasted, and donned sackcloth in mourning (Esther 4:1–3).

The Jewish people would surely be torn asunder by an evil beast, just as Joseph's brothers claimed that a wild animal had torn Joseph apart. As a result of the brothers' story, Jacob also tore his garments and dressed in sackcloth, mourning the apparent death of his favored son (Genesis 37:34). Later in the story, Joseph, then viceroy of Egypt, demanded that the brothers bring Benjamin down to Egypt if they wanted to procure food during the famine in Canaan. The brothers convinced their father to let Benjamin go, promising to protect him with their lives. However, once in Egypt, Joseph would ultimately test his brothers by having a royal goblet placed in Benjamin's bag, claiming that he stole it. He would see how his brothers who feigned his death would react when the life of his brother Benjamin, Rachel's other son, was on the line. The brothers immediately rent their garments, knowing that they had not protected Joseph's younger brother, even though he was only their half brother (Genesis 44:1–13).

The irony that rests at the heart of this narrative sequence is powerful. The brothers caused much pain to Joseph and Benjamin, resulting in the tearing of their father's garments, but in the end they tore their own garments because of the pain they felt in not fulfilling their father's oath to protect their younger brother (Benjamin, and implicitly, originally Joseph). It demonstrated just how far they had come; they now not only internalized what they had done both to Joseph and to their father, Jacob, but also truly anguished over Benjamin's predicament.

It is not surprising, then, that years later, Mordechai, who was a descendant of the tribe of Benjamin, would rend his garments and don sackcloth when the lives of his brothers and sisters, the progeny of the twelve tribes, were threatened. Mordechai, a Benjaminite, reciprocated the response to his ancestor's peril. We also recognize that in every generation the text addresses us, as Jews, who identify with the threat to Jewish life in general.[4]

When Esther was informed that Mordechai had torn his garments and sat in mourning, she was greatly distressed and sent more appropriate clothing for Mordechai to wear so that he could enter the palace to see her (Esther 4:4).[5] She felt that her cousin and guardian, enjoying a connection to the royal court through her, need not experience embarrassment for any reason. Mordechai, however, refused the garments, feeling that if his people were in peril, he could not wear the garments of pretense. He would not enter the royal palace and pay homage to the ruler who would destroy his people.

As we reflect upon Mordechai's reaction to his people's distress, how many of us, seeing others suffering, show our pain?

Do we identify with the suffering of others so that our own pain is as evident as our outward apparel, or do we believe that our status, position, or circumstances make us inured to any suffering? In another vein, do our garments of royalty protect us, or are we "one of the people," *achad ha-am*, sharing not only the past but also the future?

Without speaking a word, Mordechai attracted Esther's attention through the garments he wore. The garments of mourning were an intimation of the violence and chaos that simmered beneath the veneer of the beauty and wealth of the palace in which she lived.

When Mordechai then sent a message to Esther about the king's edict to destroy the Jewish people and charged her to go to the king and reveal that she was a Jew, Esther was reticent. She feared entering the king's presence without being summoned. Mordechai then warned her that she shouldn't think that she would escape, even if she were a part of the royal palace. If she kept silent, she and her father's house would surely perish, while deliverance would come to her people from some other source. And he added, "Who knows, perhaps you have come to be part of royalty at this moment for just such a crisis" (Esther 4:8–14). God's name is manifestly missing here, and there doesn't seem to be a clear sense of providence in Mordechai's remarks, assuring her that God will save her and her people. All he could tell her was "Who knows?" Esther would have to act without any firm guarantees that her people would survive.[6]

Esther Approaches the King in Her Royal Garb

Although Mordechai could not envelop Esther with a mantle of promise and surety, nevertheless she instructed her cousin to have all the Jews in Shushan join her in fasting and praying for three days, as she and her maidens prepared to go before King Ahasuerus. On the third day, Esther put on royal garments and entered the inner court of the palace (Esther 4:15–17). Just as the priests had to don their vestments to enter the Temple, and especially the inner courtyard, coming close to the Holy of Holies, the inner sanctum, and the Divine Presence, so, too, Esther had to envelop herself in the garments that, according to the tradition, embodied the *Ru'ach ha-Kodesh*, the Holy Spirit.[7]

Esther's royal garments gave her a façade of power and authority that was necessary as she presented herself publicly. The link between clothing and political power is something we witness every day in politics and that has always been apparent in human life. As an illustration, note Caroline Weber's book, *Queen of Fashion: What Marie Antoinette Wore to the Revolution*,[8] a biography of Marie Antoinette and a history of eighteenth-century France through the lens of her choices of clothing. What Weber emphasizes is that Marie Antoinette spent much of her energy stirring up controversy and making political statements through the garments she wore. She went from her early years at Versailles, in which she was constantly criticized for breaches in sartorial etiquette, to an unpopular queen who attempted to create an air of power through her choice of clothes. Everyone hated her because of her Austrian descent, but she would show them that she was an independent, strong individual. To this end, as an example, she wore men's riding clothes and rode astride, which was very uncommon at the Court of Versailles, where women rode sidesaddle in beautiful feminine outfits. She had a portrait painted of her in her riding gear and had copies sent to all the courts of Europe. She seemed to want to reinvent herself as a powerful king and used clothing to provoke the public and convince people that she had power.

Weber points out that clothing has always been a vehicle to send political messages, and it is no different today. During the presidential election of 2008, Cindy McCain, wife of Republican presidential hopeful John McCain, wore a highly conservative Oscar de la Renta outfit that cost some $300,000 to the National Republican Convention. Michelle Obama, wife of Barack Obama, on the other hand, chose a twenty-one-year-old designer, Jason Wu, to design her Inaugural Ball gown, which was consistent with the message of her husband—we are going to support small businesses and help the little guy, the average American. The message was clear: I am comfortable in J. Crew clothing, and I'm just like you, as is my husband, whose administration is accessible and egalitarian.[9]

Interestingly, in describing the royal garments that Esther wore, the text actually says that Esther "wore kingship" (*tilbash malchut*), when we would have expected it to read, "Esther dressed in royal garments" (Esther 5:1). The royal garments, made up of beautiful robes, a train of pure gold, and the finest of ornaments, may have masked the anxiety she must have felt as she stood in the inner courtyard,[10] waiting for the king to extend his scepter, inviting her to approach his throne. Nevertheless, the clothing both symbolized her position as queen and underscored the new identity she had assumed; she now acted forcefully, as befits both the queen of the palace and the leader and protector of her people.

Almost all of us have had experiences in which we had to approach an authority figure to make an unwelcomed request, to stand up for what we believed was right, or even to challenge an important decision. In such cases, we could identify with the anxiety Esther felt going before the throne to speak for her people. In so doing, like her, we may have had to reveal something of ourselves that we had managed to conceal for years. It is surely not easy to confront authority, let alone challenge it, but Esther teaches us that there are times when we must muster all the strength we have and overcome the voice in us that cautions to beware of consequences.

It is no coincidence that biblically Esther's actions followed three days of spiritual preparation, as we also see in other biblical incidents, such as the revelation at Sinai and Jonah's three days in the whale. Often human beings need time to muster enough strength to enter the corridors of power and challenge it. In this regard, the tradition emphasizes that redemption is effected by three days of preparation on the part of the people. In Esther's case, it also involved wrapping herself in the spirit of her ancestors for protection.[11]

Changing Mordechai's Status

As the story unfolds, King Ahasuerus found out that Mordechai had saved the king's life by uncovering a plot to kill him. As a result, unbeknownst to Haman, the king decided to honor Mordechai and then asked Haman to suggest a way to honor a man whom the king thought was deserving. Presuming that the king planned to honor him, Haman proposed that the man should wear the king's royal garb, including the king's crown, as he was paraded on the king's horse through the city square. At that point, the king ordered Haman to dress Mordechai in the royal garb and honor him by leading him on horseback through the city, proclaiming, "This is what is done for the man whom the king wants to honor" (Esther 6:7–11).

According to one thrust of the tradition, Mordechai initially refused to dress in the royal garb, claiming that he was not ready to abandon the sackcloth he had worn for three days and don the purple garments of royalty. The transition was simply too fast. It is said that he told Haman, "Do you not know that I have worn sackcloth with ashes because of that which you have planned to do to me and to my people? How can I possibly don royal garments without washing myself?" So Haman had to take Mordechai to the bathhouse and was forced to wash him, trim his hair, and then dress him in the royal garments. And when Mordechai didn't have the strength to mount the horse himself, Haman suffered the indignity of having the Jew whom he despised stand on his back to mount the horse.[12] Mordechai needed time to prepare himself for the change in both his circumstance and his position that the donning of the king's clothing and crown symbolized.

The change in Mordechai's identity that is represented by the switch from sackcloth to royal garb is paralleled in numerous stories in the Bible. In Jonah, for example, the Ninevites covered themselves with sackcloth and the king removed his royal robe and also wore sackcloth as part of their repentance from sin and desire to change (Jonah 3:5–8). Changing garments is indeed an essential vehicle for the transformation of identity, as we learn in many other places, such as Jacob's directive to his household to rid themselves of the alien gods in their midst by purifying themselves and changing their clothing (Genesis 35:2). Clothes are synonymous with actions, beliefs, and role.[13]

An excellent example of the significance of changing one's garments as it signifies the essential change in the person himself is apparent in the Rabbis' interpretation of Psalm 30 as a whole, which is understood as referring to the Esther story. At the conclusion of the psalm, which describes the shift from persecution, suffering, and near death to rejoicing, the psalmist writes, "You turned my lament into dancing, you undid my sackcloth and girded me with joy, that [my] whole being might sing hymns to You endlessly; O Adonai, my God, I will praise You forever" (Psalm 30:12).[14]

As we consider the biblical examples where change in clothing signifies the transformation of the identity of the characters, we should be aware that there are innumerable examples of this symbolism in most cultures and throughout literature. George Orwell's *Animal Farm*,[15] an allegorical novella satirizing events leading up to and during the Stalin era, tells of a revolution of the animals on Manor Farm in England. A wise old pig, Old Major, before he dies, foments the revolt when he tells his barnyard comrades that they all can enjoy peace, prosperity, and the benefits of the farm if they overthrow the owner, Mr. Jones, and run the farm themselves. After the revolution succeeds, led by the most intelligent among them, the pigs, they erect a sign at the farm's entrance that reads "Animal Farm." They then pass a constitution of seven commandments to differentiate themselves from their previous masters. Two of the commandments state that no animal shall sleep in a bed and none shall wear clothes.

All goes well until strife breaks out among the leading pigs and a pig named Napoleon takes over. The pigs move into Jones's house and live in luxury while the other animals work their hoofs and paws to the bone. The pigs begin to trade with humans, and in time they become more and more like the humans they overthrew. They not only walk upright on two legs and entertain humans at dinners, but they also wear clothing. By wearing human garments and acting like them, they take on all the human qualities of those who saw them as merely animals. Napoleon declares that Manor Farm should be the proper name for their successful business enterprise, and he replaces the Animal Farm sign with a Manor Farm sign. Life goes on with the human pigs in full control.[16]

Let us then as readers reflect on the things that characterize essential changes in our own lives. What new garments have we recently donned that are the result of a significant change in our own life situations? Have we taken on roles that essentially changed us? And are we insightful enough to even begin to see the changes that have taken place?

After Haman paraded Mordechai through the city, Mordechai returned to the king's gate (Esther 6:12). According to the Rabbis, he resumed his former position, putting on sackcloth, because his prayers for his people's survival had not yet been answered. His people still suffered.[17] He could not wear the royal garments, indicating his own elevation, unless his people were uplifted.

Meanwhile, Haman returned home with his head covered (in Hebrew, he was *chafui rosh*) as a sign of mourning (Esther 6:12). *Chafah* does mean "to cover," but the meaning is intensified when we realize that the similar verbs *chafar* and *charaf* mean "to shame" and "to revile."[18] Note, for example, Psalm 34:6: "Let their faces not blanch" (using the verb *chafar*). Simply put, Haman was shamed and disgraced.

Subsequently, following Esther's revelation that it was Haman who sought the death of all the Jews, Haman's face was also covered (*chafu*) in shame (Esther 7:8).[19] Ironically, Haman is described as "wearing [he was literally 'covered in'] his shame," though in reality his shame was uncovered. Note, in this regard, Isaiah's comment about an idolatrous Israel, "Your nakedness shall be uncovered, and your shame shall be seen" (Isaiah 47:3). Both covering and uncovering can reveal much about what a character is feeling and experiencing.

Mordechai Wears Royalty; the Jews Are Saved

Haman was put to death by order of King Ahasuerus, and Mordechai was designated to take his place in the palace. Mordechai was second only to the king, and his assumption of power was symbolized by his wearing five royal vestments (*levush malchut*): blue and white robes, a gold crown, a mantle of fine linen and purple wool, as well as the king's ring, which had been worn by Haman (Esther 8:2, 8:15).[20] It was as if Mordechai were enveloped by royalty (*malchut*) itself as he underwent this drastic life change, not unlike the change in identity that his cousin, Esther, and perhaps the entire Jewish people in Persia had experienced.

Mordechai, according to the Rabbinic tradition, became in effect the king of the Jews.[21] To accentuate his assuming royal authority, the Rabbis added that the crown and apparel that were placed upon him were actually worn by King Ahasuerus on the day of his coronation.[22] The Rabbis marvel at the suddenness of the change in Mordechai's position and identity, noting, "Yesterday, 'he put on sackcloth with ashes' (Esther 4:1); today, 'Mordechai went forth from the presence of the king in royal apparel of blue and white' (Esther 8:15)."[23]

One wonders how Mordechai experienced his meteoric rise to power and the reversal of his and the Jewish people's fortunes. It perhaps forces us to think about similar abrupt changes in our lives and positions and how we adjusted to them. If the change were for the good, did we easily embrace it, or did we have pangs of the imposter syndrome, harboring guilt and doubts about whether we were deserving or capable of our newly acquired status? Was there an element of fear that as quickly as we moved up the ladder, we could conceivably descend?

The premonition that a sudden change for the worse in the situation of the Jewish people could occur as easily as did their reversal of fortune is hinted at by the choice of words used to describe the royal mantle with which Mordechai was covered—it was a *takhrikh* of fine linen and purple. Although designating a robe or cloak, *takhrikh* is generally thought of as a shroud. Even as Mordechai assumed a position of great power in Persia, he surely understood the vagaries of Jewish life and must have feared that such a time of security, peace, and recognition would not last forever. Such a continuous time of tranquility would only be experienced in the messianic age.

Nevertheless, at least for the moment, the Jews of Persia, just as the Jews in other periods of Jewish history such as the Golden Age in Spain, could rejoice and delight in their lives. The light shone for Israel, while her enemies were shrouded in darkness.[24] In this regard, we resonate with the words of the Scroll of Esther: "The city of Shushan rang with joyous cries. The Jews enjoyed light and gladness, happiness and honor" (Esther 8:15–16). These are the very words used in the first part of the *Havdalah* ceremony, marking the distinction between Shabbat and the rest of the week. Each week, on the Sabbath, which is described by the Rabbis as "a day of all light" (*yom she-kulo 'or*), we have a taste of the messianic era, the time of perfection in which we will experience the light of the Divine. Isaiah states, "Arise and shine for your light has dawned; the Presence of Adonai has shown upon you. Behold, darkness shall cover the earth, and thick clouds the peoples; but upon you Adonai will shine" (Isaiah 60:1–2).

Purim: Concealing and Revealing

The garments that enveloped Adam and Eve in the Garden, the *katnot 'or*, garments made not just of skin (*'or*) but also of light (*'or*), and that they wore as they left Eden and then handed down to their progeny, now adorned Mordechai, Esther, and the entire Jewish people. As a result, the Jews were commanded to mark this moment of survival and transformation, these days of light, in every generation by celebrating the holiday of Purim. Every year on the fourteenth and fifteenth of the Hebrew month of

Adar, Jews all over the world celebrate this paradigmatic event in Jewish history in which things as they seem to be are overturned. Darkness and persecution are transformed into light and hope.

On Purim, Jews dress up and wear masks that change faces etched in pain and suffering into joy and frivolity. On the surface, it seems that Purim involves an escape from reality, one moment in which we can mask the pain and difficulties we experience and don fanciful carnival masks and costumes. All is turned on its head on Purim; even gender roles are ignored, and men and women can dress up as the other.

Yet in a deeper way, this Jewish carnival experience allows us to challenge the inevitability of things as they are, inherited identities and fates.[25] And in so doing, Purim provides us with the hope that the garments we put on that seem only to mask our present realities can reveal the deep-seated consciousness of our potential for change, our ability to bring happiness and fulfillment to our lives.

Purim's masks may seem to conceal, if just for a moment, the chaos and pain of our present lives and enable us to escape this reality, but they may really offer us the chance to don serious masks of conscious determination to bring the light of the Divine into our world.[26] Yes, God may not be mentioned in the entire book of Esther, and some have seen this as an intimation of the existence of sheer chaos in the world, where anarchy is at play.[27] Yet, we must ask what lies beneath a story that intimates the absence of God and meaning, and the holiday of Purim, which is about frivolity and play.

Underneath the garment of the story is perhaps a glimpse of the existence of a force in the universe that can help us move beyond who we are and what our lives presently are, and enable us to become who we aspire to be. What may be necessary is for us to recognize that, unlike the Exodus story, in which God is recognized through redemptive miracles, the Purim story demands that we come to recognize the Presence of the Divine through the ability to hear the hidden voice of God. The redemptive paradigm of Esther is to see the camouflaged Divine in the darkness of our lives.[28] Purim bespeaks the existence in the world of the light of the Divine, sparks of which are hidden beneath the surface of our lives, and ours is the task to sew those sparks into a full garment of splendor that will enhance the majesty of our souls. Perhaps that is the reason why Maimonides stated that "all prophetic books and sacred writings will cease to be read in the messianic era except the book of Esther."[29]

Epilogue

The Jews of Persia, according to the Scroll of Esther, experienced the light of redemption and rejoiced in it. They were enveloped by the very light of the Divine with which God created the world. In the beginning, the Divine was wrapped in a garment of light, and the entire world from end to end became resplendent with its brightness, as the psalmist writes, "Covered with light as with a garment, You spread the heavens like a tent cloth" (Psalm 104:2).[1] According to the Rabbis, God even wore the heavens and earth themselves like garments, having created prior worlds and having discarded them like worn-out clothing. The Divine put on and took off these garments, changing them until God created a world with which God was satisfied.[2]

In a tradition cited in chapter 1, God was pictured as wearing seven different garments at various points in Israelite history, from creation to the coming of the Messiah.[3] In the human realm there are people for whom clothes are becoming, but their actual garments are not comely, while others have clothes that are comely, but they themselves are not. Their characters are not reflected in the clothes they wear.[4] In contrast, the garments worn by God are always becoming, ever synonymous with the divine essence, which is manifested in different ways at different times.[5] The garments fit each moment to ensure Israel's ever-evolving relationship with God. This, therefore, was the guarantee that one day a messianic figure would appear who himself would be adorned in garments of light.

Each of us must then ask whether the garments we place upon ourselves match who we are, or is there an essential disconnect between what we wear, which we think enhances us, and our core characters? Does our metaphoric clothing mask what lies underneath and are we conscious of it at all? Perhaps some of us wear a mask of bravado, self-confidence, and even power, though we are aware of our own frailty and weakness.

Although we are flawed, God nevertheless depends on us. According to the Rabbinic tradition, if the Messiah is to come, God needs the Jewish people to fulfill its role as the covenanted partner of the Divine. God is dependent upon Israel, through its observance of the commandments, to make God manifest in the world.

According to the Rabbis, the love relationship between God and Israel was apparent in God's calling Israel God's bride in ten passages in Scripture, most of which are found in the Song of Songs. Corresponding to these verses, some Rabbinic commentators state that Israel in turn adorned God by describing the Divine as wearing not seven but ten garments. The purpose of God wearing these garments, symbolizing characteristics such as righteousness, strength, glory, and majesty, was to enable Israel to survive its enemies, but more so, to fulfill God's commandments, which Israel wore like the ornaments of a bride.[6]

There are numerous biblical verses that contain descriptions of God wearing these essential characteristics as clothing, all of which culminate with God donning garments of triumph. Isaiah, for example, states, "[God] donned victory like a coat of mail, with a helmet of triumph on His head; He clothed Himself with garments of retribution, wrapped Himself in zeal as in a robe" (Isaiah 59:17).

In the end, Israel, too, will be dressed in triumphal garb, representing its survival and the fulfillment of the covenant. Isaiah also notes, in this regard, that one day Israel will declare, "I greatly rejoice in Adonai, my whole being exults in God; for He has clothed me with garments of salvation [*yesha*], wrapped me in a robe of victory, like a bridegroom adorned in a turban; like a bride bedecked in her finery" (Isaiah 61:10). The bridegroom will cover his bride with garments of salvation and righteousness, and both will rejoice in the fulfillment of their relationship.[7]

The coming to fruition of the covenant between God and humanity will surely usher in the messianic age. The Rabbis portray God adorning the Messiah with the last of the divine garments, the garment of salvation described by Isaiah. And the splendor of the garment, made up of divine light, will stream forth from one end of the world to the other, and Israel will bask in the light.[8]

The light worn by God in creating the world and used by God to cover Adam and Eve when they left the Garden will one day be worn by the Messiah and will again radiate from one end of the earth to the other.[9]

In an alternative tradition, God is pictured as covering the Messiah with seven canopies of precious stones and pearls, from which will flow the four rivers that originally emanated from Eden (Genesis 2:10–14)—one of wine, one of honey, one of milk, and the last of balsam. And the Holy One will embrace the Messiah and bring him under the canopy where all the righteous of the generations will be gathered.[10]

However, not all are destined to be enhanced by the light of the Divine. From the very beginning of Creation, light was prepared and intended only for the righteous.[11] According to the psalmist, "Light is sown for the righteous" (Psalm 97:11), and the Rabbinic tradition generally takes this literally—it was planted in the Garden of Eden and is hidden there until the messianic era, when it will shine forth upon them, as Isaiah states, "Arise, shine forth, for your light has come" (Isaiah 60:1).[12]

Another midrashic tradition interprets this verse to mean that righteous individuals continually sow the light of Creation, only to gather its yield in the World to Come. They observe the commandments of Torah and then ultimately reap their reward.[13] God's light is embodied in the actions of the righteous of every generation.[14]

The light of Creation, therefore, was sewn metaphorically into the garments that were handed down from generation to generation, and one day they will adorn the righteous in the World to Come. The promise that all righteous people will eventually be enveloped by God's light is kept alive in each generation by those who themselves don garments of righteousness and majesty, and each and every human being has the opportunity to wear those garments and hand them down to their progeny.

Acknowledgments

As the prophet Elijah and his disciple Elisha approached the Jordan River, Elijah took his mantle, rolled it up, and struck the water, thereby dividing the water so that they could cross on dry land. Elijah then asked Elisha, "What can I do for you before God takes me from you?" Elisha replied, "Let a double portion of your spirit rest upon me." As they were walking, a fiery chariot appeared and Elijah was taken up to heaven in a whirlwind. Elisha picked up the mantle that had dropped from Elijah, and like Elijah, he struck the water of the Jordan and once again it parted, and Elisha crossed over. The spirit of Elijah had surely settled upon Elisha (2 Kings 2:8–15).

According to one Rabbinic tradition, the Jordan was divided into two separate paths, providing both Elijah and Elisha a way to cross over. The river was so divided due to the merit of each (*Me'am Lo'ez* to 2 Kings 2:8). Up to this point, Elisha was simply linked to his master, but here, for the first time, his individuality was manifest. Elisha would soon set out on his career path as a prophet to Israel.

And after Elijah's ascension to heaven, Elisha himself struck the waters of the Jordan, and they miraculously parted. Elisha learned well from his teacher and now had the ability to cross the Jordan on his own. The Rabbis even suggest that Elisha's miracle surpassed that of Elijah, because it was only Elisha's power that divided the Jordan once Elijah had died (*Yalkut Shimoni*, vol. 1, *remez* 92).

This is the story of every teacher-student, every mentoring relationship. It is first incumbent upon students to internalize the wisdom and experiences of their teacher. Yet, they ultimately must come to their own individual understanding and application of the knowledge they have garnered. The irony is that it is only by going beyond that which they have learned that students truly preserve the teaching and importance of those who were their teachers. Only in this way is the *shalshelet ha-kabbalah*, the chain of tradition from Sinai, extended by the addition of new, vibrant links.

During my thirty-seven years of teaching and service at Hebrew Union College–Jewish Institute of Religion (HUC-JIR) I have been blessed with several generations of wonderful students, who have added immeasurably to my life. The opportunity to share my passion for the texts of our past and, in particular, the wonderful world of florid Rabbinic biblical interpretation called midrash with interested, intelligent, and committed students has truly been a blessing. There has never been a moment in which I did not eagerly anticipate every opportunity to share my own search for meaning as a Jew and as a human being with our rabbinical, cantorial, and education students, as well as with committed laypeople in the Jewish community.

When Elijah was told by God to anoint Elisha as his successor, he threw his mantle over him, thereby sharing his core identity as a prophet of God with his young disciple. Frequently in the Bible, the passing on of garments is symbolic of the transfer of authority, but it also involves the transferring of the spirit of the Divine, present to human beings since the days of Adam and Eve in the Garden of Eden. This, then, is the essence of my experience as a teacher at Hebrew Union College—to share my sense that God's Presence, however defined, is apparent in each and every moment we immerse ourselves in Jewish texts and imbibe the power of its words, which are suffused with *kedushah*, holiness. It is in this spirit that I dedicate this book to my students, who have enabled me to continue to reap the rewards of Torah study.

Among the many students I've been privileged to teach over the years, I particularly want to thank Rabbi Emma Gottlieb, who serves Temple Bnai Israel in Plattsburgh, New York. A graduate of the New York School in 2010, Emma was my research assistant during the summer of 2009 and helped immensely in jump-starting this project.

Rav Nachman b. Isaac asked, "Why are the words of Torah likened to a tree, as it is said: 'It is a tree of life to those who grasp it' [Proverbs 3:18]? This is to teach us that just as a small tree may ignite a bigger tree; so, too, it is with students of Torah—the younger sharpen the minds of the older." This coheres with what Rabbi Chanina said: "I have learned much from my teachers, and from my colleagues more than my teachers, but from my disciples more than from them all" (Babylonian Talmud, *Ta'anit* 7a).

I have also learned much and benefited from the staff at Jewish Lights Publishing. It has been a wonderful blessing for me for nearly two decades to be associated with Stuart M. Matlins, founder and publisher of Jewish Lights. I was privileged to be a part of the visioning that led to the creation of this publishing company, which has had a major impact on both Jewish life and myriad individuals in the wider community. And it was due to his caveat that the books published by Jewish Lights should spiritually, emotionally, and personally enhance their readers that I felt challenged to find a voice to bring my passion and teaching of the Bible and midrash to as wide an audience as possible. Without Stuart's encouragement and support, I most probably would not have ventured to bring my teachings beyond the seminary walls and the academic community to a broader spectrum of people who, like myself, are searching for meaning. I am also indebted to others at Jewish Lights, chief among them Emily Wichland, whose insights, wise suggestions, and prodding have made this work, like my previous ones, immeasurably better. I am also grateful to Debra Corman, whose eye for grammar and style, and meticulous reading, has moved this work forward to publication.

It is, therefore, with a sense of gratefulness that I pass on this work to you, the reader. I personally have gained much from my own immersion into the biblical texts involving clothing, and it is my hope that as you engage with the stories, passages, and interpretations included in the volume, you, too, will find an enhanced sense of your own identity and interactions with others. May you be enlightened by the process of uncovering the garments of Torah; may you be warmed and sustained by their light.

Notes

Preface

1. "The Emperor's New Clothes," Hans Christian Andersen, Plot, *Wikipedia*, p. 1.
2. Ibid., p. 2.
3. Quotations from the Hebrew Bible are drawn or adapted from the *JPS Hebrew-English Tanakh* (Philadelphia: Jewish Publication Society, 1999).
4. *Zohar* 111:152a, as translated by Daniel Matt, *Zohar: Annotated & Explained* (Woodstock, VT: SkyLight Paths, 2002), p. 5.
5. Michael Fishbane, *The Garments of Torah: Essays in Biblical Hermeneutics* (Bloomington: Indiana University Press, 1992), p. 35.
6. This acronym was probably introduced in Moses de Leon's *Sefer ha-Pardes*, which itself is no longer extant, but was cited in *Raya Me'emna* and in *Tikkunei Zohar*. See my *The Way Into Torah* (Woodstock, VT: Jewish Lights, 2000), pp. 78–91.
7. See *Midrash Ottiyyot d'Rabbi Akiba* and *Bemidbar Rabbah* 13:15.
8. Susan Handelman, *The Slayers of Moses: The Emergence of Rabbinic Interpretation in Modern Literary Theory* (Albany: State University of New York Press, 1982), p. 75.
9. Erich Auerbach, "Odysseus' Scar," in *Mimesis: The Representation of Reality in Western Literature* (Princeton, NJ: Princeton University Press, 1953), p. 9.

10. Daniel Boyarin, *Intertextuality and the Reading of Midrash* (Bloomington: Indiana University Press, 1990), pp. 40–41.

Introduction

1. Animism is the attribution of living soul and power to plants, inanimate objects, and natural phenomena.

2. Rachel Kemper, *Costume* (New York: Newsweek Books, 1977), p. 7.

3. Ibid., p. 9. See also Alison Lurie, *The Language of Clothes* (New York: Henry Holt, 1981), pp. 29–31.

4. Lurie, *Language of Clothes*, p. 4.

5. Elizabeth Wilson, *Adorned in Dreams: Fashion and Modernity* (London: Virago Press, 1985), p. 11.

6. "The Apparel Oft Proclaims the Man," *The Bard Spot*, Wednesday, January 14, 2009.

7. Kemper, *Costume*, pp. 154–164.

8. Lori Hope Lefkovitz, *In Scripture: The First Stories of Jewish Sexual Identities* (Lanham, MD: Rowan & Littlefield, 2010), p. 62. The author utilizes an important analysis of the Superman story by Harry Brod, "Of Mice and Supermen: Images of Jewish Masculinity," in *Gender and Judaism: The Transformation of Tradition*, ed. Tamar Rudafsky (New York: New York University Press, 1975), pp. 279–93.

9. Emma Tarlo, *Clothing Matters: Dress and Identity in India* (Chicago: The University of Chicago Press, 1996), p. 17.

10. Ibid., p. 1. Tarlo notes that the term "costume" separates clothes from the individuals who wear them.

11. Lurie, *Language of Clothes*, p. 1.

12. Susan B. Kaiser, *The Social Psychology of Clothing: Symbolic Appearances in Context* (New York: Fairchild Publications, 1998), p. 182.

13. Sheryl Gay Stolberg, "White House Unbuttons Formal Dress Code," *New York Times*, January 28, 2009.

14. Geoff Earle, "Photo op 'chelle game,'" *New York Post*, October 4, 2011, p. 9.
15. Andrew Malcolm, "Top of the Ticket," *Los Angeles Times*, April 7, 2010.
16. Tarlo, *Clothing Matters*, pp. 8, 17.
17. Lurie, *Language of Clothes*, p. 212.
18. Jay Michaelson, "Revealing Ourselves through Our Masks," *Forward*, March 5, 2004.
19. Kemper, *Costume*, p. 14.
20. Lurie, *Language of Clothes*, p. 115.
21. The term "sumptuary" (from *sumptus*) pertains to regulating expenditures and lavishness.
22. Lurie, *Language of Clothes*, p. 115.
23. Kemper, *Costume*, p. 8.
24. Tarlo, *Clothing Matters*, xx–xxi.
25. Ibid., p. 18.
26. Ibid., pp. 13–15.
27. Ibid., p. 52.

1. Divine Garments of Creation: Concealing Our Nakedness, Revealing Our Inner Core

1. This is based on Psalm 104:1: "Wrapped in a robe of light, You spread the heavens like a tent cloth." See, e.g., *Midrash Tanchuma ha-Nidpas, Parashat Vayakhel* 4.
2. *Bereshit Rabbah* 3:4, 15:22.
3. See Ibn Ezra and *Metzudat David* to Psalm 104:2; *Pirkei d'Rabbi Eliezer*, chap. 3. Perhaps we already see here an implicit play on 'or (with an *alef*), meaning "light," and 'or (with an *ayin*), meaning "[animal] skin."
4. *Pesikta d'Rav Kahana* 22:5; *Pesikta Rabbati* 37:12; *Midrash Tehillim* 93:1; and *Yalkut ha-Makhiri* to Isaiah 61:10 and Psalm 93:1. The number of garments in these parallel traditions at times deviates from the dominant tradition of seven.

5. For example, Isaiah 59:17, where God is said to don retribution, victory, and salvation.

6. See *Pesikta Rabbati* 37:2, among others. See also the epilogue, p. 159.

7. See the sources cited in note 4 above.

8. The Rabbis portray Adam and Eve as covered with either light (*'or*, with an *alef*) or a kind of skin (*'or*, with an *ayin*) of nail, which protected them in the Garden. There is an inherent wordplay between the Hebrew for "light" and "skin." In some texts, a cloud of glory (*anan kavod*) is said to cover them. See, in this regard, note 9 below and several parallels in *Pirkei d'Rabbi Eliezer*, chap. 14.

9. E.g., *Midrash ha-Gadol* to Genesis 3:7.

10. *Pirkei d'Rabbi Eliezer*, chap. 14.

11. Richard Goodwin, *A Voice of the Sixties: Remembering America* (Boston: Little, Brown, 1988), pp. 267–271.

12. Ibid., p. 270.

13. The phrase for "uncovering nakedness" in Hebrew is frequently a version of *gilui ervah*. See other similar prophetic examples, including Ezekiel 23:10, Isaiah 47:2–3, and Hosea 2:11.

14. Walter Brueggemann, *Isaiah*, Westminster Bible Companion (Louisville, KY: Westminster John Knox Press, 1998).

15. Avivah Gottlieb Zornberg, *The Murmuring Deep: Reflections on the Biblical Unconscious* (New York: Schocken Books, 2009), p. 212.

16. See any number of Rabbinic commentaries to Exodus 34:33–35, including Ibn Ezra, Rashbam, *Keli Yakar*, and Ralbag, as well as *Midrash Tanchuma Buber, Shemot* 16.

17. *Shir ha-Shirim Rabbah* 3:7.

18. See Norman J. Cohen, *Self, Struggle and Change: Family Conflict Stories in Genesis and Their Healing Insights for Our Lives* (Woodstock, VT: Jewish Lights, 1996), p. 30.

19. See, among many sources, Babylonian Talmud, *Berachot* 40a, 70a; Rashi, Abrabanel, *Torah Temimah*, Radak, and *Midrash Aggadah* to Genesis 3:7. The Rabbis also suggest other objects that Adam and Eve might have used to fashion their garments, among which is the fruit of the vine. This perhaps is an allusion to Noah's sin in Genesis 9.

20. *Bereshit Rabbah* 19:6. This interpretation is based on the sound play in Hebrew between *te'einah* (fig tree) and *te'unah* (an experience of suffering).

21. Naomi H. Rosenblatt and Joshua Horwitz, *Wrestling with Angels* (New York: Delta, 1996), p. 39.

22. For example, *Midrash Tehillim* 92:6 and Cassuto on Genesis 3:8.

23. Elie Wiesel, *Messengers of God: Biblical Portraits and Legends* (New York: Random House, 1966), p. 25. Wiesel drew the analogy of the house and the builder from texts like *The Book of Adam and Eve*, a part of the Apocrypha.

24. *Midrash ha-Gadol* to Genesis 3:8.

25. See, among many midrashic traditions, *Targum Neophiti* and *Targum Jonathan* to Genesis 3:10–11; *Bereshit Rabbah* 19:6; *Pirkei d'Rabbi Eliezer*, chap. 14; *Midrash Rabbenu Bachya* to Genesis 3:21.

26. Nehama Liebowitz, *Studies in Shemot, Parashat Tetzaveh* 2 (Israel: Ha-Omonim Press, 1993), pp. 530–31, quoting the *Akeidat Yitzchak* by R. Isaac Arama.

27. *The Book of Adam and Eve* in the Apocrypha, section 20.

28. Rosenblatt and Horwitz, *Wrestling with Angels*, p. 43. See also Sforno to Genesis 3:21.

29. The best-known text is Babylonian Talmud, *Sotah* 14a. See also *Bereshit Rabbah* 20:12, which states that it was animal skins with their wool.

30. *Pirkei d'Rabbi Eliezer*, chap. 20; *Midrash Tehillim* 92:6; *Yalkut Shimoni*, vol. 1, *remez* 34.

31. See, e.g., *Pirkei d'Rabbi Eliezer*, chap. 20; several *Targumim*, like *Targum Onkolos* to Genesis 3:21.

32. *Me'am Lo'ez* to Genesis 3:21.

33. Chizkuni to Genesis 3:21.

34. Among others, the commentary of R. Meir of Rothenberg to Genesis 3:21; *Midrash Abkir* to Genesis 3; *Midrash Rabbenu Bachya* to Genesis 3:21.

35. See *Bereshit Rabbah* 20:12, in which R. Meir is said to possess such a rendering, and *Targum Onkolos* to Genesis 3:21.

36. *Itturei Torah* to Genesis 3:18; Nehama Leibowitz, *Studies in Shemot, Parashat Tetzaveh* 2, pp. 528–30.

37. Louis Ginzberg, *The Legends of the Jews* (Philadelphia: The Jewish Publication Society, 1968), vol. 5, 103, n. 93.

38. Babylonian Talmud, *Pesachim* 54b; *Midrash ha-Gadol* and Radak to Genesis 3:21.

39. *Bereshit Rabbah* 12:6. Here, the Rabbis are playing on Psalm 139:11, "Surely, the darkness shall bruise me [*yeshufeini*]," which they identify with the serpent, about whom it is said in Genesis 3:15, "He shall bruise [*yeshufcha*] your head, and you will bruise [*teshufenu*] his heel."

40. *Pirkei d'Rabbi Eliezer*, chap. 20.

41. *Bereshit Rabbah* 12:6.

42. See Babylonian Talmud, *Berachot* 52b; Babylonian Talmud, *Pesachim* 53b; *Bereshit Rabbah* 12:6.

43. See, among other texts, *Bereshit Rabbah* 20:12 and *Yalkut Shimoni*, vol. 1, *remez* 34.

44. *Pirkei d'Rabbi Eliezer*, chap. 24; *Midrash Rabbenu Bachya* to Genesis 3:21. There are a number of parallel traditions with slightly different lists of those who possessed the garments (e.g., *Bemidbar Rabbah* 4:8).

45. Matt, *Zohar*, pp. 45–53. See also *Zohar* 1:22. For the notion that the Torah is identified with light in this context, see,

e.g., *Pesikta Rabbati* 36:1 and *Midrash of Rabbi Moshe Alshich* to Genesis 3:7.

2. Noah's Garments after the Flood: Ensuring Protection or Covering Shame?

1. Noah was called an *ish ha-adamah* (Genesis 9:20), "a man who works the ground."

2. Cassuto to Genesis 9:21.

3. See, e.g., *Targum Jonathan* to Genesis 9:20; *Pirkei d'Rabbi Eliezer*, chap. 23; *Midrash ha-Gadol* to Genesis 9:20.

4. Rashi to Genesis 9:20; *Midrash Tanchuma ha-Nidpas, Parashat Noach* 15; *Tzenah Urenah* to Genesis 9:21.

5. *Sifrei Devarim, piska* 323; Babylonian Talmud, *Berachot* 40a; Babylonian Talmud, *Sanhedrin* 70a–b, *Bemidbar Rabbah* 10:4; *Midrash Lekach Tov* and *Me'am Lo'ez* to Genesis 9:20; *Torah Temimah* to Genesis 9:21.

6. Avivah Gottlieb Zornberg, *Genesis: The Beginning of Desire* (Philadelphia: Jewish Publication Society, 1995), p. 70.

7. *Midrash Lekach Tov* to Genesis 9:20.

8. John Moscowitz, "What Kind of a Father Was Lamech?" *The Modern Men's Torah Commentary*, ed. Jeffrey K. Salkin (Woodstock, VT: Jewish Lights, 2009), p. 12.

9. Leon R. Kass, *The Beginning of Wisdom* (New York: Free Press, 2003), p. 204.

10. William Golding, *The Lord of the Flies* (Boston: Faber & Faber, 1958).

11. Kate Chopin, *The Awakening* (Chicago: H. S. Stone, 1899).

12. Rashi and Chizkuni to Genesis 9:21; *Bereshit Rabbah* 36:4.

13. See *Yalkut Shimoni*, vol. 1, *remez* 61; *Midrash ha-Gadol* to Genesis 9:22; and Radak and *Siftei Chakhamim* to Genesis 9:21.

14. Rosenblatt and Horwitz, *Wrestling with Angels*, p. 74.

15. Peter Pitzele, *Our Fathers' Wells* (San Francisco: Harper and Row, 1995), p. 72.

16. Ramban to Deuteronomy 27:20.
17. See Rashi to Genesis 9:23.
18. Sforno to Genesis 9:24.
19. Cassuto to Genesis 9:23.
20. *Yalkut Shimoni*, vol. 1, *remez* 61; Sforno to Genesis 9:23.
21. *Shemot Rabbah* 18:5.
22. *Bereshit Rabbah* 36:6.
23. *Midrash Aggadah* and *Tzenah Urenah* to Genesis 9:23.
24. *Midrash ha-Gadol, Midrash Lekach Tov*, and *Tzenah Urenah* to Genesis 9:23.
25. *Shemot Rabbah* 18:5.
26. See the comments of Ibn Ezra and *Me'am Lo'ez* on Psalm 104:1.
27. Philo, *Questions and Answers on Genesis*, book 2, no. 70.
28. *Bereshit Rabbati* to Genesis 27:15.

3. The Garments of Disguise—Am I Jacob or Esau? Revealing and Concealing Identity

1. *"Midrash Aseret Melakhim,"* in *Otzar Midrashim*, ed. J. D. Eisenstein (New York: Mishor, 1915), pp. 461–62.
2. Ginzberg, *Legends*, vol. 1, pp. 332–333.
3. *Bereshit Rabbah* 65:16 and *Siftei Chakhamim* to Genesis 27:12.
4. Rashi to Genesis 27:12; *Siftei Chakhamim* and *Peirush Yonatan* to Genesis 27:15.
5. *Sefer ha-Yashar* to *Parashat Toledot*.
6. *Yalkut Shimoni*, vol. 1, *remez* 115.
7. *Bereshit Rabbati* and *Tzenah Urenah* to Genesis 27:15.
8. *Aggadat Bereshit* 43.
9. *Pirkei d'Rabbi Eliezer*, chap. 24; *Yalkut Shimoni*, vol. 1, *remez* 115.

10. See, e.g., the review by Roger Moore in the *Orlando Sentinel*, Friday, September 16, 2011.

11. "Long Hair," *Wikipedia*.

12. *Targum Jonathan* and Radak to 1 Samuel 28:8.

13. *Bereshit Rabbah* 65:17; Sforno to Genesis 27:22; Ginzberg, *Legends*, p. 332.

14. *Midrash Aggadah* to Genesis 27:15.

15. *Targum Onkolos* to Genesis 27:15; *Bereshit Rabbah* 65:16; *Pesikta Rabbati, piska* 23/24; *Devarim Rabbah* 1:15; *Yalkut Shimoni*, vol. 1, *remez* 115; *Me'am Lo'ez* to Genesis 7:15.

16. *Bereshit Rabbah* 65:16; *Pesikta Rabbati, piska* 23/24.

17. See the *Targum*, Radak, and *Metzudat David* to Judges 6:34; Radak to 1 Chronicles 12:18; Radak and Ralbag to 1 Kings 22:10; and various commentaries to 1 Samuel 2:18.

18. See, among many sources, Rashi, *Midrash Sekhel Tov*, *Tzenah Urenah*, and *Me'am Lo'ez* to Genesis 27:27; and *Yalkut Shimoni*, vol. 1, *remez* 115.

19. Sforno and *Ba'al ha-Turim* to Genesis 27:27.

20. Radak and *Tur* to Genesis 27:27.

21. *Midrash Tanchuma Buber, Parashat Toledot* 22.

22. *Bereshit Rabbah* 65:22; *Shir ha-Shirim Rabbah* 4:11.

23. Babylonian Talmud, *Sanhedrin* 37a; *Aggadat Bereshit* 43; *Midrash Aggadah* to Genesis 27:24.

24. Maurice Samuel, *Certain People of the Book* (New York: Alfred Knopf, 1967), pp. 130–85.

25. Zornberg, *Genesis*, pp. 142, 163.

26. See, e.g., *Bereshit Rabbah* 60:15 and the Ramban to Genesis 24:65. Note, too, the comments of Ekbal Beraka, in *The Veil: A Modern Viewpoint* (Cairo: Rosel Yousef Publishing House, 2002), in which it is suggested that Islam developed the notion of women covering their faces from this passage in Genesis 24.

27. Libby Henik, "Rebecca's Veil: A Weave of Conflict and Agency," in *Answering a Question with a Question: Contemporary Psychoanalysis and Jewish Thought*, ed. Lewis Aron and Libby Henik (Boston: Academic Studies Press, 2009), pp. 272–73.

28. See Cohen, *Self, Struggle and Change*, p. 96; Zornberg, *Genesis*, pp. 159–160; and Henik, "Rebecca's Veil," pp. 276–77.

29. See Zornberg, *Genesis*, pp. 159–60, and her quotation and extension of the Maharal's comment on Genesis 25:22. Note as well in this regard how Eve leaves the Garden of Eden with a sense of who she is, with a developed sense of herself, signified by the personal name she carries—*Chavah*, "Life." This is the result of her conception of Cain and Abel. In contrast, Adam is known by the generic *ha-Adam*, "the Man."

30. Henik, "Rebecca's Veil," p. 277.

31. Zornberg, *Genesis*, pp. 167–68.

32. "*Gulliver's Travels*: Themes, Motifs & Symbols," www.sparknotes.com.

33. Zornberg, *Genesis*, p. 150.

34. Lefkovitz, *In Scripture*, pp. 48–50.

35. Zornberg, *Genesis*, p. 172.

36. Adin Steinsaltz, *Biblical Images* (Norvale, NJ: Jason Aronson, 1994), pp. 41–42.

37. Norman J. Cohen, *Voices from Genesis: Guiding Us through the Stages of Life* (Woodstock, VT: Jewish Lights, 1998), pp. 112–13.

38. Ibid.

39. Zornberg, *Genesis*, pp. 175–76.

40. Ibid., pp. 178–79.

41. *Midrash ha-Gadol* to Genesis 27:27.

42. *Midrash Tanchuma Buber, Parashat Toledot* 22; *Me'am Lo'ez* to Genesis 27:27.

43. *Midrash Bereshit Zuta* and *Midrash ha-Gadol* to Genesis 27:27.

4. Stripping Joseph of His Special Coat: A Symbol of Power and Status, a Source of Pain and Isolation

1. The coat represented Jacob's destiny even as it reminded him of the difficulty of his journey.

2. Thomas Mann, *Joseph and His Brothers*, trans. H. T. Lowe-Porter (New York: Alfred A. Knopf, 1944), p. 320.

3. Ibid., p. 323.

4. See Cohen, *Self, Struggle and Change*, p. 134.

5. Mann, *Joseph and His Brothers*, p. 320.

6. Zora Neale Hurston, *Their Eyes Were Watching God* (Urbana: University of Illinois Press, 1978).

7. "The Use of Clothing in the Novel *Their Eyes Were Watching God*," www.docshare.com.

8. The meaning of *kutonet passim* is not clear, though it clearly implies that Jacob gave Joseph a distinctive garment. See Claus Westermann, *Genesis 37–50: A Commentary*, trans. John J. Scullion (Minneapolis: Augsburg Publishing House, 1986), on this verse.

9. *Targum Neophiti* and *Midrash ha-Gadol* to Genesis 37:3. See also Ginzberg, *Legends*, vol. 5, n. 43.

10. See *Targum Neophiti* to Genesis 37:3, n. 5, in which it is compared to a *pargod*, a long-sleeved tunic. See also *Midrash Lekach Tov* to Genesis 37:3.

11. Mann, *Joseph and His Brothers*, pp. 323–24.

12. The syntax of Genesis 37:2 is very odd and could be read, "Joseph tended [guided, led] his brothers with their sheep," rather than "Joseph tended the sheep with his brothers." See Cohen, *Self, Struggle and Change*, pp. 153–54.

13. Wiesel, *Messengers*, p. 153.

14. "*The Taming of the Shrew*: Themes, Motifs & Symbols," www.sparknotes.com.

15. Cohen, *Self, Struggle and Change*, p. 154.

16. Ginzberg, *Legends*, vol. 2, p. 7; *Aggadat Bereshit* 6:13; *Midrash Lekach Tov*; Chizkuni to Genesis 37:3.

17. *Midrash ha-Gadol* to Genesis 37:3.

18. Malbim to Genesis 37:3.

19. *Aggadat Bereshit* 60:13. See also *Midrash Tehilim* 22:20 in this regard.

20. Radak to Isaiah 22:21. See also Babylonian Talmud, *Baba Kama* 11a; and *Ha-Chut ha-Meshulash* to Genesis 37:3.

21. Meir of Rothenberg to Genesis 37:23.

22. *Midrash Rabbenu Bachya* and *Keli Yakar* to Genesis 37:3.

23. See also Ramban and *Me'am Lo'ez* to Genesis 41:42.

24. *Bereshit Rabbah* 84:7; Lefkovitz, *In Scripture*, p. 89.

25. *Me'am Lo'ez* to Genesis 37:23.

26. *Bereshit Rabbah* 84:16; *Yalkut Shimoni*, vol. 1, *remez* 142; *Midrash Sekhel Tov*, Abrabanel, *Siftei Chakhamim*, and *Itturei Torah* to Genesis 37:23.

27. Ibn Ezra and the *Tur on the Torah* to Genesis 37:23; Ginzberg, *Legends*, vol. 2, p. 13.

28. Mann, *Joseph and His Brothers*, pp. 373–74; Zornberg, *Genesis*, pp. 268–69.

29. Rosenblatt and Horwitz, *Wrestling with Angels*, p. 320. See also Philo, *On Joseph*, no. 22.

30. *Bereshit Rabbah* 84:19.

31. See Rashi to Genesis 37:31.

32. Ramban, *Ha-Chut ha-Meshulash*, and *Me'am Lo'ez* to Genesis 37:32.

33. See also Philo, *On Joseph*, section 27, and Abrabanel to Genesis 37:32–33.

34. Janet Tucker, "The Religious Symbolism of Clothing in Dostoevsky's Crime and Punishment," *Fyodor Dostoevsky's Crime and Punshment*, ed. Harold Bloom (Philadelphia: Chelsea House, 2004), p. 218.

35. *Me'am Lo'ez* to Genesis 37:34; Zornberg, *Genesis*, p. 269.

36. Zornberg, *Genesis*, p. 267.

37. Tarlo, *Clothing Matters*, p. 69.

38. Babylonian Talmud, *Moed Katan* 26a–b.

39. *Bereshit Rabbah* 84:20; *Yalkut Shimoni*, vol. 1, *remez* 143; *Midrash Sekhel Tov* to Genesis 37:34.

40. Lefkovitz, *In Scripture*, p. 94, citing Qur'an 12:96.

41. This is an embellishment of *Midrash Tanchuma ha-Nidpas, Ve-yehi* 17. See Norman J. Cohen, "Surviving the Narrow Places: Judah and Joseph and the Journey to Wholeness," in *Midrash and Medicine: Healing Body and Soul in the Jewish Interpretive Tradition*, ed. William Cutter (Woodstock, VT: Jewish Lights, 2011), pp. 30–31.

42. Zornberg, *The Murmuring Deep*, p. 319.

5. Tamar Confronts Judah: Masks Can Reveal More Than They Conceal about Us

1. Judah was positioned to demand that the brothers return Joseph to their father, yet he urged that they sell him to the Ishmaelite traders. Instead of taking Joseph's life themselves, they got rid of him by selling him into slavery. See Genesis 37:26–28.

2. See Deuteronomy 25:5–10 for the biblical laws of levirate marriage.

3. Note Judah's recognition in the end that Tamar was much more righteous than he was (Genesis 38:26).

4. According to Jewish law, Tamar was perennially in a state of *zikkah*—she was literally tied to Shelah forever.

5. Ramban to Genesis 38:12.

6. Mann, *Joseph and His Brothers*, p. 1038.

7. See the creative analysis of Sandra Rapoport, *Biblical Seductions: Six Stories Retold, Based on Talmud and Midrash* (Jersey City, NJ: Ktav, 2011), pp. 184–185. Rapoport uses several key midrashic texts, chief among them *Midrash Lekach Tov* to Genesis 38:14.

8. Ibid., p. 187. See, among many texts, Rashi and *Midrash Sekhel Tov* to Genesis 38:14.

9. *Einayim* comes from the Singular *ayin*, which not only means "eye" but also "well." The place-name most probably means "Entrance to the Two Wells."

10. "Shakespeare's *King Lear* and the Nature of Disguise," www.e-mago.com.

11. "*Hamlet*: Structure, Themes, Imagery, Symbols," http:schoolworkhelper. net.

12. Rapoport, *Biblical Seductions*, p. 192, quoting Abrabanel, Chizkuni, and the Netziv on Genesis 38:14.

13. Ibn Ezra to Genesis 38:15.

14. *Bereshit Rabbati* to Genesis 38:15.

15. Mann, *Joseph and His Brothers*, p. 1039.

16. *Vayikra Rabbah* 26:7.

17. Babylonian Talmud, *Sotah* 10b; *Bereshit Rabbah* 85:8; *Yalkut Shimoni*, vol. 1, *remez* 145; Rashi, Ramban, *Midrash ha-Gadol*, the *Tur*, and *Me'am Lo'ez* to Genesis 38:15.

18. *Bereshit Rabbah* 85:7.

19. Rapoport, *Biblical Seductions*, p. 189.

20. Rapoport, *Biblical Seductions*, p. 200, quoting a number of Rabbinic traditions.

21. *Bereshit Rabbah* 85:9.

22. Zornberg, *Genesis*, pp. 326–9.

23. See Cohen, "Surviving the Narrow Places," p. 36.

24. See, among many sources, *Targum Onkolos*, Rashbam, and *Me'am Lo'ez* to Genesis 38:18.

Notes 181

25. Rashi, Kimchi, and Ramban to Genesis 38:18.
26. The *Tur*, Ramban, and *Ha-Chut ha-Meshulash* to Genesis 38:18.
27. *Midrash Rabbenu Bachya* to Genesis 38:18. The three items a husband is obliged to provide for his wife are noted in Exodus 21:10.
28. The translations add the object "them" to say that Judah recognized the three symbols of his own identity. We, as readers, realize that Judah finally came to recognize himself in the process, the core of his being.
29. This genealogy is of course seen as the messianic genealogy in both Rabbinic Judaism and Christianity.
30. *Bemidbar Rabbah* 23:6.
31. See *Metzudat David* and *Me'am Lo'ez* to Isaiah 11:5.
32. *Metzudat David* to Psalm 132:9.
33. See also in this regard Psalm 132:16.

6. Joseph and Potiphar's Wife: Uncovering True Identity

1. Zornberg, *The Murmuring Deep*, p. 297.
2. The Bible goes out of its way to describe Joseph as being well built and handsome.
3. The verse in Genesis 39:6 says that "Joseph was [*va-yehi*] attractive and handsome." The Rabbis, however, read the word *va-yehi* not in its simple meaning "Joseph was attractive," but rather "Joseph became attractive," i.e., he cultivated his good looks. See, in this regard, James Kugel, *In Potiphar's House: The Interpretive Life of Biblical Texts* (Cambridge: Harvard University Press, 1994), pp. 77–78, 125.
4. She is so named, not in the Bible, but in later midrashic texts and in the Qur'an.
5. See *Tzenah Urenah* and *Me'am Lo'ez* to this verse. See also Leibowitz, *Studies in Genesis*, p. 436.
6. *Midrash Tanchuma ha-Nidpas, Vayeishev* 5.

7. *Sefer ha-Yashar* to *Bereshit* 39; *Me'am Lo'ez* to Genesis 39:7; Ginzberg, *Legends*, vol. 2, p. 53.

8. The tradition in the midrash is that she grabbed his coat from behind, since if she stood face to face with him, she could not have grabbed him in this manner. See *Midrash Lekach Tov* and *Midrash Sekhel Tov* to Genesis 39:12. The same tradition is found in Islam, e.g., Qur'an 12:25–27.

9. *Sefer ha-Yashar* to Genesis 39:12.

10. Robert Alter, *The Art of Biblical Narrative* (New York: Basic Books, 1981), p. 109.

11. Westermann, *Genesis 37–50* to Genesis 39:13–15.

12. See James Kugel's creative analysis of this passage in his important work, *In Potiphar's House*, pp. 97–98.

13. *Aggadat Bereshit*, chap. 64.

14. Isaac Arama, *Akeidat Yitzhak* to Genesis 39:10.

15. *Itturei Torah* to Genesis 39:11.

16. *Bereshit Rabbah* 87:8.

17. Babylonian Talmud, *Sotah* 36b; *Bereshit Rabbah* 87:7; *Midrash Rabbenu Bachya* to Genesis 39:8.

18. *Itturei Torah* to Genesis 39:12.

19. *Tzenah Urenah* to Genesis 39:11; Leibowitz, *Studies in Genesis*, to Genesis 39:12. According to Ramban's comment on Genesis 39:12, because Joseph did not want to use force to take the coat from her, he actually took off the garment and left it with her.

20. Westermann, *Genesis 37–50* to Genesis 39:13–15.

21. See *Bereshit Rabbati* to Genesis 39:15.

22. *Bereshit Rabbah* 87:8; *Midrash ha-Gadol, Midrash Sekhel Tov*, and *Me'am Lo'ez* to Genesis 39:16.

23. Mann, *Joseph and His Brothers*, pp. 830–31.

24. Lefkovitz, *In Scripture*, p. 93.

25. For example, *The History of al-Tabari* trans. Franz Rothenthal (Albany: SUNY Press, 1989), vol. 2, no. 381–82.

26. Philo, *On Joseph*, no. 52.
27. Samuel, *Certain People of the Book*, p. 330.
28. *Itturei Torah* to Genesis 39:16.
29. Daniel Matt, *Zohar* (Mahwah, NJ: Paulist Press, 1983), pp. 89–90.
30. "Imagery and Symbolism: Disguise and Seeming," *Measure for Measure Study Guide*, www.crossref-it.info/textguide.
31. Pitzele, *Our Fathers' Wells*, p. 212; Rosenblatt and Horwitz, *Wrestling with Angels*, p. 333.
32. See Cohen, *Self, Struggle and Change*, pp. 170–71.
33. *Bereshit Rabbah* 90:3; *Vayikra Rabbah* 23:9; *Bemidbar Rabbah* 14:6.
34. *Kanaf* can also mean "corner" and is used to refer to the four corners of a tallit as well as the four corners of the world.
35. Edward F. Campbell Jr., ed., *Ruth: A New Translation with Introduction, Notes, and Commentary*, The Anchor Bible (Garden City, NY: Doubleday, 1975), p. 123.
36. See Rapoport, *Biblical Seductions*, p. 479, especially her citation of *Mishbatzot Zahav* to Ruth 3:7.
37. See the commentaries to Ezekiel 16, which stress that the metaphor in this passage is one of marriage, e.g., Radak and *Metzudat David* to Ezekiel 16:8.
38. The key phrase is *eirom ve-eryah*, in which the word *eirom* is understood not simply as *arum*, "naked," meaning "uncovered," but rather "unprotected," because they sinned and did not observe God's command. The first example of this particular emphasis on the term *eirom* is found in Deuteronomy 28:45–48, in which it is used in relationship to Israel not observing the commandments.
39. See, e.g., *Pirkei d'Rabbi Eliezer*, chap. 14.
40. See Radak's comment on this passage that God adorned Israel with thirteen different items, which parallel the thirteen indignities that Israel suffered in Egypt.

41. Deuteronomy 22:12 and, of course, the third portion of the traditional *Sh'ma* taken from Numbers 15.

42. There is a wonderful play on words here as the Rabbis interpret the phrase "they shall strip you of your clothing" (Ezekiel 16:39). The word "your clothing" (*begadayikh*) can also be vocalized to read "your treacheries," reading not *beged*, "clothes," but rather *bagad*, "betray."

43. Midrash on Exodus 33:6 in *Shemot Rabbah* 25:2.

44. Among several parallel sources, see *Mekhilta d'Rabbi Ishmael, Massekhta d'Beshallach* to Exodus 14:15; *Yalkut Shimoni*, vol. 1, *remez* 146; and *Midrash ha-Gadol* to Genesis 39:12.

45. Babylonian Talmud, *Sotah* 13a–b; *Mekhilta d'Rabbi Ishmael, Massekhta d'Beshallach* to Exodus 13:19.

46. W. Gunther Plaut, *The Torah: A Modern Commentary* (New York: UAHC, 1981), p. 485, n. 24, quoting *Torat ha-Moreh*.

7. Aaron's Death and the Symbolism of the Priestly Garments: Vehicles of Holiness and Transformation

1. See, e.g., the comments of Rabbi Meir of Rothenberg to Leviticus 8:13.

2. When Moses placed the priestly garments on Aaron's sons in Leviticus 8:13, the Bible uses the words *va-yalbisheim kutanot*, the same expression used in Genesis 3:21.

3. Rashi to Ezekiel 42:14.

4. Babylonian Talmud, *Zevachim* 17b.

5. *Vayikra Rabbah* 21:12.

6. Eliyahu Munk, trans., *Midrash Rabbeinu Bachya, Torah Commentary*, vol. 4 (Jerusalem: Urim, 1998), p. 1280.

7. Tennessee Williams, *A Streetcar Named Desire*, ed. Martin Browne (London: Penguin, 1993).

8. "Symbolic Devices in Tennessee Williams, *A Streetcar Named Desire*," www.english-literature.uni-bayreuth.

9. Rashi, *Metzudat David*, and *Me'am Lo'ez* to Isaiah 63:2–3.

10. The Wisdom of Ben Sira, purporting to describe life in Jerusalem in the third to second century BCE, is a part of the Apocrypha, the books that did not find their way into the Hebrew Bible. See R. H. Charles, *The Apocrypha and Pseudepigrapha of the Old Testament*, vol. 1 (Oxford: Clarenden Press, 1971), pp. 507–508.

11. The translation is drawn from *Service of the Synagogue: Day of Atonement* (New York: Hebrew Publishing Co., 1959).

12. Wisdom of Ben Sira 50:11.

13. See Rashi's comment on Exodus 28:3.

14. See Nehama Leibowitz's extension of the Malbim's comment on Exodus 28:2, in which he plays on the repetition of God's command, "Thou shall make holy garments ... to sanctify [them]." One command was given to Moses himself; the other was directed to skilled workers. See Leibowitz, *Studies in Exodus, Parashat Tetzaveh*, p. 532. There are two types of vestments, external and internal. See also Or ha-Chayyim on the same verse in this regard.

15. "*The Canterbury Tales*: Themes, Motifs & Symbols," www.sparknotes.com/lit.

16. Ramban to Exodus 28:4.

17. *Midrash Rabbenu Bachya* and Isaac Arama, *Akeidat Yitzchak on the Torah,* on Exodus 28:4. Both quote Babylonian Talmud, *Arakhin* 16a. They emphasize that the biblical section describing the garments (Exodus 28) is placed right next to the one dealing with the sacrifices (Exodus 29:12). See also Babylonian Talmud, *Zevachim* 88b; Palestinian Talmud, *Yoma* 7:5; and *Vayikra Rabbah* 10:6.

18. *Midrash Moshe Alshich* on Exodus 28:4. The multiple layers of garments worn by the High Priest during his service in the Temple is not unlike the multiple layers of vestments worn by Catholic, Anglican, Lutheran, and other clergy when presiding over liturgical functions.

19. See Leviticus 6:4, e.g., which is the passage most midrashim and commentators focus on in this regard.

20. Leviticus 16:23; Ezekiel 42:14; Babylonian Talmud, *Yoma* 12b; *Vayikra Rabbah* 21:12.

21. Babylonian Talmud, *Yoma* 23b; Babylonian Talmud, *Shabbat* 114a.

22. Radak to Ezekiel 42:14.

23. There is an alternative biblical tradition that Aaron died at Moserah (Deuteronomy 10:6), which seems to be identical with Moserot in Numbers 33:30. According to Josephus, *Antiquities* 4.4.7, and several Arab sources, Aaron died in Petra. To this day, pilgrims visit Aaron's tomb on the summit of Jebel Harun.

24. Numbers 20:26, 28. The verses read literally: "Moses stripped Aaron … (and) his garments." See also the comment by Or ha-Chayyim.

25. Note the comments in *Midrash Tanchuma ha-Nidpas, Parashat Chukkat* 16; *Midrash Tanchuma Buber, Parashat Chukkat* 40; *Bemidbar Rabbah* 19:19; and *Yalkut Shimoni,* vol. 1, *remez* 764.

26. *Midrash Rabbenu Bachya* to Numbers 20:28.

27. See Ginzberg's translation, in his *Legends of the Jews,* vol. 3, p. 324, of this beautiful interchange found in *Midrash Petirat Aharon.*

28. This is very much similar to the common folkloristic motif of the Magic Garment, which produces invulnerability. See Motif D 1344.9.1 in the Aarne-Thompson, *Motif Index of Folk Literature,* 6 vols. (Bloomington: Indiana University Press, 1955–58).

29. See a poignant passage in the the Wisdom of Solomon 18:24–25, part of the Apocrypha, in Charles, *The Apocrypha and Pseudepigrapha,* vol. 1, p. 566.

30. See, e.g., *Midrash Aggadah* to Numbers 20:27 and Ibn Ezra to the previous verse.

31. Sforno to Numbers 20:26.

32. *Midrash ha-Gadol* to Numbers 20:28, as well as Ramban and the *Tur* to Numbers 20:26.

33. *Midrash Rabbenu Bachya* to Numbers 20:28.

34. *Midrash Petirat Aharon* in *Otzar Midrashim*, ed. Eisenstein, vol. 1, pp. 12–15.

35. Rashi to Numbers 20:25; *Bemidbar Rabbah* 19:17, 19. The midrash adds that the righteous are informed of the day of their death so that they can bequeath their crowns to their children.

36. *Yalkut Shimoni*, vol. 1, *remez* 764.

37. Rashi to Numbers 20:25. See, especially, the Christian Syriac version of Aaron's death, *Mimro d'al Aharon Kahana*, by the famous church father Jacob of Serugh, who includes Eleazar kissing the garments he received from his father.

38. *Siftei Chakhamim* to Numbers 20:26. In *Sifra d'bei Rav* 41a, which is part of the *Mekhilta d'Milluim*, the Rabbis note that in effect Moses served as Aaron's priestly assistant, dressing and undressing him, a role he would also play with Eleazar.

39. *Ba'al ha-Turim* to Numbers 20:21.

40. *Siftei Chakhamim* to Numbers 20:26.

41. *Midrash Lekach Tov* to Numbers 20:28.

42. *Yalkut Shimoni*, vol. 1, *remez* 764; *Tzenah Urenah* to Numbers 20:25.

43. *Me'am Lo'ez* to Numbers 20:26.

44. *Yalkut Shimoni*, vol. 1, *remez* 515; and *Midrash ha-Gadol* to Numbers 20:24.

45. Ginzberg, *Legends*, vol. 6, n. 637.

46. *Midrash Lekach Tov* to Numbers 20:26.

47. Ramban to Numbers 20:26, and n. 211 and the citation of *Sifra, Tzav* 1:6.

48. *Midrash ha-Gadol* to Numbers 20:24. In *Midrash Petirat Aharon* and in other sources, including the Muslim scholar al-Tabari, we learn that his burial site is unknown.

49. *Shir ha-Shirim Rabbah* 4:5; *Bemidbar Rabbah* 19:20.

50. *Midrash Lekach Tov* to Numbers 20:29.

51. *Bemidbar Rabbah* 19:20.

52. *Torah Temimah* to Numbers 20:26, citing Babylonian Talmud, *Mo'ed Katan* 28a, and *Itturei Torah* on the same verse.

8. David Dons Saul's Armor: Wearing Our Own Garments, Embracing Our Own Identity

1. V. P. Lang, *The Reign and Rejection of King Saul* (Cambridge, UK: SBL, 1989), p. 156.

2. Rashi, Radak, and M. Segel, *Sifrei Shmuel* to 1 Samuel 15:27.

3. Lang, *Reign and Rejection of King Saul*, pp. 156–63.

4. See pp. 94–96.

5. Among several parallel comments, see Kimchi's comment to 1 Samuel 15:27 and *Midrash Tehillim* 57:3.

6. 1 Samuel 24:20 as understood in *Me'am Lo'ez* and Kimchi to 1 Samuel 15:27.

7. Segel, *Sifrei Shmuel* to 1 Samuel 15:27.

8. Some Rabbinic authorities claimed that it was Jeroboam's garment that was torn, though the clear consensus is that Ahijah tore his own garment. See, e.g., *Ruth Rabbah* 7:12.

9. *Ruth Rabbah* 7:12; Kimchi to 1 Samuel 15:27; *Yalkut Shimoni*, vol. 1, *remez* 123.

10. *Midrash Shmuel* 18:5.

11. Or ha-Chayyim to Numbers 14:6.

12. Kaiser, *Social Psychology of Clothing*, pp. 195–196.

13. *Me'am Lo'ez* to 1 Samuel 17:38.

14. Segel, *Sifrei Shmuel* to 1 Samuel 17:39.

15. Erica M., "Macbeth and the Clothes That Make the Man," www.teenink.com/college guide.

16. See *Yalkut Shimoni*, vol. 2, *remez* 127; and Rashi and *Me'am Lo'ez* to 1 Samuel 17:38. Some of these passages stress that miraculous change occurred when an individual was anointed king.

17. *History of Al-Tabari*, vol. 3, no. 555. Similarly, some Rabbinic sources suggest that David in effect was anointed as king and at that David grew into Saul's armor. See, e.g., Rashi to 1 Samuel 17:38.

18. *Vayikra Rabbah* 26:9; *Midrash Tanchuma Buber, Emor* 6; *Midrash Shmuel*, chap. 21.

19. Rashi to 1 Samuel 17:38, among others.

20. Segel, *Sifrei Shmuel* to 1 Samuel 18:4.

21. Homer, *The Iliad*, trans. Richmond Lattimore (Chicago: University of Chicago Press, 1951), book 6, section 235.

22. *Me'am Lo'ez* to 1 Samuel 18:4.

23. William McKane, *1 & 2 Samuel* (London: SCM Press, 1963), to 1 Samuel 18:4.

24. "*Hamlet* Symbolism, Imagery and Allegory," www.shmoop.com.

25. *Metzudat David* to 1 Samuel 19:23; Isaiah d'Trani to 1 Samuel 19:24.

26. Babylonian Talmud, *Berachot* 62b; *Midrash Tehillim* 56; Segal, *Sifrei Shmuel* to 1 Samuel 24:4.

27. See, e.g., *Me'am Lo'ez* to Samuel 24:4.

28. See above in this chapter and on p. 96.

29. 1 Kings 1:1 as quoted and interpreted in *Me'am Lo'ez* to 1 Samuel 24:5.

30. *Vayikra Rabbah* 26:2; *Bemidbar Rabbah* 19:2.

31. The so-called "Song of the Bow" was thought to have been recorded in *Sefer ha-Yashar* mentioned in Joshua 10:13.

32. Babylonian Talmud, *Mo'ed Katan* 26a. The Rabbis applied these symbols to the death of Rabbinic leaders of their day, like the *Nasi* and *Av Bet Din*.

9. Elijah and Elisha—Transferring the Prophet's Mantle: Passing on Authority, Wearing It in Individual Ways

1. *Metzudat David* on 2 Kings 2:8; The Anchor Bible to 2 Kings 2:8, trans Mordechai Cogan and Hayim Tadmor (New York: Doubleday, 1964), n. 20; A. J. Rosenberg, ed., *2 Kings: A New English Translation* (New York: Judaica Press, 1980) to 2 Kings 2:18.

2. See *Pirkei d'Rabbi Eliezer*, chap. 31; and *Yalkut Shimoni*, vol. 2, *remez* 224, among many parallel sources.

3. Apparently, the hairy mantle first became associated with Elijah in intertestamental literature and later was picked up by the Rabbis. See The Anchor Bible to 2 Kings 1:8, n. 20, and Rabbinic commentary on the same verse, including *Metzudat David* and Hartum.

4. Martin Buber, *The Prophetic Faith* (New York: Harper and Row, 1960), p. 76.

5. See various commentaries to 1 Kings 19:13, including Hartum.

6. See also Radak and *Metzudat David* to 1 Kings 19:13.

7. Ralbag to 1 Kings 19:19.

8. Hartum and The Anchor Bible to 1 Kings 19:19, trans. Mordechai Cogan (New York: Doubleday, 1964).

9. "Bride Wears 127-Year-Old Wedding Dress," *Inside Edition*, September 1, 2011, www.insideedition.com.

10. *Me'am Lo'ez* to 1 Kings 19:19. Perhaps the interpretation that he merely touched him with the corner of his garment is based on the actual wording in the verse—he cast his mantle "toward him" (*eilav*), rather than "upon him" (*alav*).

11. "Odysseus: A Greek Epic Hero," in *Reports & Essays: Literature—Plays*, www.studyworld.com.

12. *Pesikta Rabbati* 4:2.

13. For many more parallels, see *Pesikta Rabbati* 4:2 and *Yalkut Shimoni*, vol. 2, *remez* 209.

14. *Me'am Lo'ez* to 2 Kings 2:8.

15. *Berit Olam* to 2 Kings 2:7–8.

16. Radak's comments to Babylonian Talmud, *Mo'ed Katan* 22b; and Rosenberg's translation of 2 Kings 2:12 and his notes.

17. Hartum and *Me'am Lo'ez* to 2 Kings 2:13.

18. *Devarim Rabbah* 10:3. Some midrashic texts use the parting of the Red Sea to draw the parallel between Elisha and Moses. See, e.g., *Pesikta d'Rav Kahana* 1:4.

19. *Yalkut Shimoni*, vol. 1, *remez* 92; Rashi, Radak, and Rosenberg to 2 Kings 2:14.

20. Note the insightful comment in *Berit Olam* to 2 Kings 2:12–18.

21. *Midrash Lekach Tov* to Numbers 20:25.

10. Esther, Mordechai, and Haman: Change of Garments; Change of Identity

1. Note the comments in Babylonian Talmud, *Chullin* 139b on Deuteronomy 31:18. See also the poignant interpretation in Zornberg, *The Murmuring Deep*, pp. 108–9.

2. "Symbolism in John Steinbeck's *The Chrysanthemums* Essay," http://mybestessays.com.

3. Michaelson, "Revealing Ourselves."

4. *Esther Rabbah* 8:1.

5. *Kohelet Rabbah* 4:17.

6. Zornberg, *The Murmuring Deep*, p. 124.

7. Babylonian Talmud, *Megillah* 4b.

8. Caroline Weber, *Queen of Fashion: What Marie Antoinette Wore to the Revolution* (New York: Henry Holt, 2006).

9. "The Link between Clothing and Politics," http://video. ezinemark.com.

10. *Esther Rabbah* 9:1.

11. *Bereshit Rabbah* 56:1.

12. *Vayikra Rabbah* 28:6; *Esther Rabbah* 10:4; *Pirkei d'Rabbi Eliezer*, chap. 50.

13. See the comments of Rashi, Ibn Ezra, Or ha-Chayyim, and *Midrash Rabbenu Bachya*, among others, to Genesis 35:2.

14. See Rashi's comments on this verse.

15. George Orwell, *Animal Farm* (New York: Harcourt, Brace, 1946).

16. Michael J. Cummings, "Animal Farm: A Study Guide," www.cummingsstudyguides.net.

17. *Esther Rabbah* 10:6; *Shemot Rabbah* 38:4.

18. For example, see Jeremiah 50:12; Isaiah 24:23, 37:23, and 47:3.

19. See also *Pirkei d'Rabbi Eliezer*, chap. 50.

20. *Bemidbar Rabbah* 14:8.

21. *Bereshit Rabbah* 87:6; *Esther Rabbah* 10:12; *Pirkei d'Rabbi Eliezer*, chap. 50.

22. *Pirkei d'Rabbi Eliezer*, chap. 50; *Kohelet Rabbah* 5:2. Even the horse upon which Mordechai rode when he was led through the city by Haman was the very horse that the king had ridden on his coronation day.

23. *Shir ha-Shirim Rabbah* 6:12.

24. *Midrash Tehillim* 22.

25. Lefkovitz, *In Scripture*, p. 120.

26. Michaelson, "Revealing Ourselves."

27. Zornberg, *The Murmuring Deep*, pp. 108, 116.

28. Ibid., p. 131.

29. Ramban, *Hilkhot Purim* 218.

Epilogue

1. *Shemot Rabbah* 50:1.
2. See a number of commentaries on Psalm 102:27, including *Metzudat David.*
3. See also *Pesikta d'Rav Kahana* 22:8.
4. *Midrash Tehillim* 24:1.
5. *Midrash Tehillim* 93:1.
6. *Devarim Rabbah* 2:36; *Shir ha-Shirim Rabbah* 4:10.
7. See the comments to this Isaiah verse from Radak, drawing on *Targum Jonathan* on the verse and *Metzudat David,* as well as Brueggemann, *Isaiah.*
8. *Pesikta Rabbati* 37:2.
9. *Pesikta Rabbati* 36:2, 37:2; *Midrash Tehillim* 27:1.
10. *Pesikta Rabbati* 37:1.
11. Babylonian Talmud, *Ta'anit* 15a.
12. See *Vayikra Rabbah* 11:7; *Midrash Tanchuma ha-Nidpas, Shemini* 9; and *Shemot Rabbah* 35:1.
13. *Me'am Lo'ez* to Psalm 97:11.
14. *Bereshit Rabbah* 1:6.

Suggested Further Readings

Altar, Robert. *The Art of Biblical Narrative*. New York: Basic Books, 1981.

Cohen, Norman J. *Hineini in Our Lives: Learning How to Respond to Others through 14 Biblical Texts & Personal Stories*. Woodstock, VT: Jewish Lights Publishing, 2003.

———. *Moses and the Journey to Leadership: Timeless Lessons of Effective Management from the Bible and Today's Leaders*. Woodstock, VT: Jewish Lights Publishing, 2007.

———. *Self, Struggle & Change: Family Conflict Stories in Genesis and Their Healing Insights for Our Lives*. Woodstock, VT: Jewish Lights Publishing, 1995.

———. *Voices from Genesis: Guiding Us through the Stages of Life*. Woodstock, VT: Jewish Lights Publishing, 1998.

———. *The Way Into Torah*. Woodstock, VT: Jewish Lights Publishing, 2000.

De La Haye, Amy, and Elizabeth Wilson. *Defining Dress: Dress as Object, Meaning and Identity*. Manchester, UK: Manchester University Press, 1999.

Fishbane, Michael. *The Garments of Torah: Essays in Biblical Hermeneutics*. Bloomington: Indiana University Press, 1992.

Kaiser, Susan. *The Social Psychology of Clothing: Symbolic Appearances in Context*. New York: Fairchild Publications, 1998.

Kemper, Rachel. *The History of Costume*. New York: Newsweek Books, 1977.

Kugel, James. *In Potiphar's House: The Interpretive Life of Biblical Texts*. Cambridge: Harvard University Press, 1992.

Lefkovitz, Lori Hope. *In Scripture: The First Stories of Jewish Sexual Identities*. Lanham, MD: Rowman & Littlefield Publishers, 2010.

Leibowitz, Nehama. *Studies in the Weekly Sidra*. Jerusalem: W.Z.O., Department for Torah Education and Culture in the Diaspora, 1958.

Lurie, Alison. *The Language of Clothes*. New York: Henry Holt and Company, 1981.

Mann, Thomas. *Joseph and His Brothers*. Translated by H. T. Lowe-Porter. New York: Alfred Knopf, 1944.

Rapoport, Susan. *Biblical Seductions: Six Stories Retold, Based on Talmud and Midrash*. Jersey City, NJ: Ktav Publishing House, 2011.

Roach-Higgens, Mary Ellen, Joanne Eicher, and Kim Johnson, eds. *Dress and Identity*. New York: Fairchild Publishers, 1995.

Tarlo, Emma. *Clothing Matters: Dress and Identity in India*. Chicago: University of Chicago Press, 1996.

Weber, Caroline. *Queen of Fashion: What Marie Antoinette Wore to the Revolution*. New York: Henry Holt and Company, 2006.

Wilson, Elizabeth. *Adorned in Dreams: Fashion and Modernity*. London: Virago Press, 1985.

Zornberg, Aviva. *Genesis: The Beginning of Desire*. Philadelphia: Jewish Publication Society, 1995.

———. *The Murmuring Deep: Reflections on the Biblical Unconscious*. New York: Schocken Books, 2009.

Bar/Bat Mitzvah

The Mitzvah Project Book
Making Mitzvah Part of Your Bar/Bat Mitzvah ... and Your Life
By Liz Suneby and Diane Heiman; Foreword by Rabbi Jeffrey K. Salkin; Preface by Rabbi Sharon Brous
The go-to source for Jewish young adults and their families looking to make the world a better place through good deeds—big or small.
6 x 9, 224 pp, Quality PB Original, 978-1-58023-458-0 **$16.99** *For ages 11–13*

The JGirl's Guide: The Young Jewish Woman's Handbook for Coming of Age
By Penina Adelman, Ali Feldman and Shulamit Reinharz
6 x 9, 240 pp, Quality PB, 978-1-58023-215-9 **$14.99** *For ages 11 & up*
The JGirl's Teacher's and Parent's Guide 8½ x 11, 56 pp, PB, 978-1-58023-225-8 **$8.99**
The Bar/Bat Mitzvah Memory Book, 2nd Edition: An Album for Treasuring the Spiritual Celebration *By Rabbi Jeffrey K. Salkin and Nina Salkin*
8 x 10, 48 pp, 2-color text, Deluxe HC, ribbon marker, 978-1-58023-263-0 **$19.99**

For Kids—Putting God on Your Guest List, 2nd Edition: How to Claim the Spiritual Meaning of Your Bar or Bat Mitzvah *By Rabbi Jeffrey K. Salkin*
6 x 9, 144 pp, Quality PB, 978-1-58023-308-8 **$15.99** *For ages 11–13*
Putting God on the Guest List, 3rd Edition: How to Reclaim the Spiritual Meaning of Your Child's Bar or Bat Mitzvah *By Rabbi Jeffrey K. Salkin*
6 x 9, 224 pp, Quality PB, 978-1-58023-222-7 **$16.99**; HC, 978-1-58023-260-9 **$24.99**
Putting God on the Guest List Teacher's Guide
8½ x 11, 48 pp, PB, 978-1-58023-226-5 **$8.99**
Tough Questions Jews Ask, 2nd Edition: A Young Adult's Guide to Building a Jewish Life
By Rabbi Edward Feinstein 6 x 9, 160 pp, Quality PB, 978-1-58023-454-2 **$16.99** *For ages 11 & up*
Tough Questions Jews Ask Teacher's Guide 8½ x 11, 72 pp, PB, 978-1-58023-187-9 **$8.95**

Bible Study/Midrash

Sage Tales: Wisdom and Wonder from the Rabbis of the Talmud
By Rabbi Burton L. Visotzky Illustrates how the stories of the Rabbis who lived in the first generations following the destruction of the Jerusalem Temple illuminate modern life's most pressing issues. 6 x 9, 256 pp, HC, 978-1-58023-456-6 **$24.99**
The Modern Men's Torah Commentary: New Insights from Jewish Men on the 54 Weekly Torah Portions *Edited by Rabbi Jeffrey K. Salkin*
6 x 9, 368 pp, HC, 978-1-58023-395-8 **$24.99**

The Genesis of Leadership: What the Bible Teaches Us about Vision, Values and Leading Change *By Rabbi Nathan Laufer; Foreword by Senator Joseph I. Lieberman*
6 x 9, 288 pp, Quality PB, 978-1-58023-352-1 **$18.99**
Hineini in Our Lives: Learning How to Respond to Others through 14 Biblical Texts and Personal Stories *By Rabbi Norman J. Cohen, PhD* 6 x 9, 240 pp, Quality PB, 978-1-58023-274-6 **$16.99**
A Man's Responsibility: A Jewish Guide to Being a Son, a Partner in Marriage, a Father and a Community Leader *By Rabbi Joseph B. Meszler* 6 x 9, 192 pp, Quality PB, 978-1-58023-435-1 **$16.99**
Moses and the Journey to Leadership: Timeless Lessons of Effective Management from the Bible and Today's Leaders *By Rabbi Norman J. Cohen, PhD*
6 x 9, 240 pp, Quality PB, 978-1-58023-351-4 **$18.99**; HC, 978-1-58023-227-2 **$21.99**

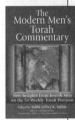

Righteous Gentiles in the Hebrew Bible: Ancient Role Models for Sacred Relationships
By Rabbi Jeffrey K. Salkin; Foreword by Rabbi Harold M. Schulweis;
Preface by Phyllis Tickle 6 x 9, 192 pp, Quality PB, 978-1-58023-364-4 **$18.99**
The Wisdom of Judaism: An Introduction to the Values of the Talmud
By Rabbi Dov Peretz Elkins 6 x 9, 192 pp, Quality PB, 978-1-58023-327-9 **$16.99**

Or phone, fax, mail or e-mail to: **JEWISH LIGHTS Publishing**
Sunset Farm Offices, Route 4 • P.O. Box 237 • Woodstock, Vermont 05091
Tel: (802) 457-4000 • Fax: (802) 457-4004 • www.jewishlights.com
Credit card orders: (800) 962-4544 (8:30AM–5:30PM EST Monday–Friday)
Generous discounts on quantity orders. SATISFACTION GUARANTEED. Prices subject to change.

Spirituality/Crafts

Jewish Threads: Hands-On Guide to Stitching Spiritual Intention into Jewish Fabric Crafts *By Diana Drew with Robert Grayson*
Learn how to make your own Jewish fabric crafts with spiritual intention—a journey of creativity, imagination and inspiration. Thirty projects.
7 x 9, 288 pp, 8-page color insert, b/w illus., Quality PB Original, 978-1-58023-442-9 **$19.99**

(from SkyLight Paths, Jewish Lights' sister imprint)

Beading—The Creative Spirit: Finding Your Sacred Center through the Art of Beadwork *By Wendy Ellsworth*
Invites you on a spiritual pilgrimage into the kaleidoscope world of glass and color.
7 x 9, 240 pp, 8-page full-color insert, b/w photos and diagrams, Quality PB, 978-1-59473-267-6 **$18.99**

Contemplative Crochet: A Hands-On Guide for Interlocking Faith and Craft *By Cindy Crandall-Frazier; Foreword by Linda Skolnik*
Will take you on a path deeper into your crocheting and your spiritual awareness.
7 x 9, 208 pp, b/w photos, Quality PB, 978-1-59473-238-6 **$16.99**

The Knitting Way: A Guide to Spiritual Self-Discovery
By Linda Skolnik and Janice MacDaniels
Shows how to use knitting to strengthen your spiritual self.
7 x 9, 240 pp, b/w photos, Quality PB, 978-1-59473-079-5 **$16.99**

The Painting Path: Embodying Spiritual Discovery through Yoga, Brush and Color *By Linda Novick; Foreword by Richard Segalman*
Explores the divine connection you can experience through art.
7 x 9, 208 pp, 8-page full-color insert, b/w photos, Quality PB, 978-1-59473-226-3 **$18.99**

The Quilting Path: A Guide to Spiritual Self-Discovery through Fabric, Thread and Kabbalah *By Louise Silk* Explores how to cultivate personal growth through quilt making. 7 x 9, 192 pp, b/w photos, Quality PB, 978-1-59473-206-5 **$16.99**

The Scrapbooking Journey: A Hands-On Guide to Spiritual Discovery
By Cory Richardson-Lauve; Foreword by Stacy Julian
Reveals how this craft can become a practice used to deepen and shape your life.
7 x 9, 176 pp, 8-page full-color insert, b/w photos, Quality PB, 978-1-59473-216-4 **$18.99**

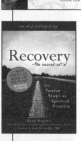

Travel

Israel—A Spiritual Travel Guide, 2nd Edition: A Companion for the Modern Jewish Pilgrim *By Rabbi Lawrence A. Hoffman, PhD*
Helps today's pilgrim tap into the deep spiritual meaning of the ancient—and modern—sites of the Holy Land.
4¾ x 10, 256 pp, Illus., Quality PB, 978-1-58023-261-6 **$18.99**
Also Available: **The Israel Mission Leader's Guide** 5½ x 8½, 16 pp, PB, 978-1-58023-085-8 **$4.95**

Twelve Steps

Recovery—The Sacred Art: The Twelve Steps as Spiritual Practice
By Rami Shapiro; Foreword by Joan Borysenko, PhD
Draws on insights and practices of different religious traditions to help you move more deeply into the universal spirituality of the Twelve Step system.
5½ x 8½, 240 pp, Quality PB Original, 978-1-59473-259-1 **$16.99**
(A book from SkyLight Paths, Jewish Lights' sister imprint)

100 Blessings Every Day: Daily Twelve Step Recovery Affirmations, Exercises for Personal Growth & Renewal Reflecting Seasons of the Jewish Year *By Rabbi Kerry M. Olitzky; Foreword by Rabbi Neil Gillman, PhD* 4½ x 6½, 432 pp, Quality PB, 978-1-879045-30-9 **$16.99**

Recovery from Codependence: A Jewish Twelve Steps Guide to Healing Your Soul
By Rabbi Kerry M. Olitzky 6 x 9, 160 pp, Quality PB, 978-1-879045-32-3 **$13.95**

Twelve Jewish Steps to Recovery, 2nd Edition: A Personal Guide to Turning from Alcoholism & Other Addictions—Drugs, Food, Gambling, Sex...
By Rabbi Kerry M. Olitzky and Stuart A. Copans, MD; Preface by Abraham J. Twerski, MD
6 x 9, 160 pp, Quality PB, 978-1-58023-409-2 **$16.99**

Women's Interest

Women, Spirituality and Transformative Leadership
Where Grace Meets Power
Edited by Kathe Schaaf, Kay Lindahl, Kathleen S. Hurty, PhD, and Reverend Guo Cheen
A dynamic conversation on the power of women's spiritual leadership and its emerging patterns of transformation.
6 x 9, 288 pp, Hardcover, 978-1-59473-313-0 **$24.99**

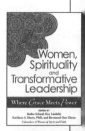

Spiritually Healthy Divorce: Navigating Disruption with Insight & Hope
by Carolyne Call A spiritual map to help you move through the twists and turns of divorce. 6 x 9, 224 pp, Quality PB, 978-1-59473-288-1 **$16.99**

New Feminist Christianity: Many Voices, Many Views
Edited by Mary E. Hunt and Diann L. Neu
Insights from ministers and theologians, activists and leaders, artists and liturgists who are shaping the future. Taken together, their voices offer a starting point for building new models of religious life and worship.
6 x 9, 384 pp, HC, 978-1-59473-285-0 **$24.99**

New Jewish Feminism: Probing the Past, Forging the Future
Edited by Rabbi Elyse Goldstein; Foreword by Anita Diamant
Looks at the growth and accomplishments of Jewish feminism and what they mean for Jewish women today and tomorrow. Features the voices of women from every area of Jewish life, addressing the important issues that concern Jewish women.
6 x 9, 480 pp, Quality PB, 978-1-58023-448-1 **$19.99**; HC, 978-1-58023-359-0 **$24.99***

Bread, Body, Spirit: Finding the Sacred in Food
Edited and with Introductions by Alice Peck 6 x 9, 224 pp, Quality PB, 978-1-59473-242-3 **$19.99**

Dance—The Sacred Art: The Joy of Movement as a Spiritual Practice
by Cynthia Winton-Henry 5½ x 8½, 224 pp, Quality PB, 978-1-59473-268-3 **$16.99**

Daughters of the Desert: Stories of Remarkable Women from Christian, Jewish and Muslim Traditions
by Claire Rudolf Murphy, Meghan Nuttall Sayres, Mary Cronk Farrell, Sarah Conover and Betsy Wharton
5½ x 8½, 192 pp, Illus., Quality PB, 978-1-59473-106-8 **$14.99** Inc. reader's discussion guide

The Divine Feminine in Biblical Wisdom Literature
Selections Annotated & Explained
Translation & Annotation by Rabbi Rami Shapiro; Foreword by Rev. Cynthia Bourgeault, PhD
5½ x 8½, 240 pp, Quality PB, 978-1-59473-109-9 **$16.99**

Divining the Body: Reclaim the Holiness of Your Physical Self
by Jan Phillips 8 x 8, 256 pp, Quality PB, 978-1-59473-080-1 **$16.99**

Honoring Motherhood: Prayers, Ceremonies & Blessings
Edited and with Introductions by Lynn L. Caruso 5 x 7¼, 272 pp, HC, 978-1-59473-239-3 **$19.99**

Next to Godliness: Finding the Sacred in Housekeeping
Edited by Alice Peck 6 x 9, 224 pp, Quality PB, 978-1-59473-214-0 **$19.99**

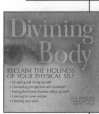

ReVisions: Seeing Torah through a Feminist Lens
by Rabbi Elyse Goldstein 5½ x 8½, 224 pp, Quality PB, 978-1-58023-117-6 **$16.95***

The Triumph of Eve & Other Subversive Bible Tales
by Matt Biers-Ariel 5½ x 8½, 192 pp, Quality PB, 978-1-59473-176-1 **$14.99**

White Fire: A Portrait of Women Spiritual Leaders in America
by Malka Drucker; Photos by Gay Block 7 x 10, 320 pp, b/w photos, HC, 978-1-893361-64-5 **$24.95**

Woman Spirit Awakening in Nature: Growing Into the Fullness of Who You Are
by Nancy Barrett Chickerneo, PhD; Foreword by Eileen Fisher
8 x 8, 224 pp, b/w illus., Quality PB, 978-1-59473-250-8 **$16.99**

Women of Color Pray: Voices of Strength, Faith, Healing, Hope and Courage
Edited and with Introductions by Christal M. Jackson
5 x 7¼, 208 pp, Quality PB, 978-1-59473-077-1 **$15.99**

The Women's Torah Commentary: New Insights from Women Rabbis on the 54 Weekly Torah Portions *Edited by Rabbi Elyse Goldstein*
6 x 9, 496 pp, Quality PB, 978-1-58023-370-5 **$19.99**; HC, 978-1-58023-076-6 **$34.95***

* A book from Jewish Lights, SkyLight Paths' sister imprint

Holidays/Holy Days

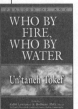

Who by Fire, Who by Water—Un'taneh Tokef
Edited by Rabbi Lawrence A. Hoffman, PhD
Examines the prayer's theology, authorship and poetry through a set of lively essays, all written in accessible language.
6 x 9, 272 pp, HC, 978-1-58023-424-5 **$24.99**

All These Vows—Kol Nidre
Edited by Rabbi Lawrence A. Hoffman, PhD
The most memorable prayer of the Jewish New Year—what it means, why we sing it, and the secret of its magical appeal.
6 x 9, 288 pp, HC, 978-1-58023-430-6 **$24.99**

Rosh Hashanah Readings: Inspiration, Information and Contemplation
Yom Kippur Readings: Inspiration, Information and Contemplation
Edited by Rabbi Dov Peretz Elkins; Section Introductions from Arthur Green's These Are the Words
Rosh Hashanah: 6 x 9, 400 pp, Quality PB, 978-1-58023-437-5 **$19.99**; HC, 978-1-58023-239-5 **$24.99**
Yom Kippur: 6 x 9, 368 pp, Quality PB, 978-1-58023-438-2 **$19.99**; HC, 978-1-58023-271-5 **$24.99**

Jewish Holidays: A Brief Introduction for Christians
By Rabbi Kerry M. Olitzky and Rabbi Daniel Judson
5½ x 8½, 176 pp, Quality PB, 978-1-58023-302-6 **$16.99**

Reclaiming Judaism as a Spiritual Practice: Holy Days and Shabbat
By Rabbi Goldie Milgram   7 x 9, 272 pp, Quality PB, 978-1-58023-205-0 **$19.99**

Shabbat, 2nd Edition: The Family Guide to Preparing for and Celebrating the Sabbath
By Dr. Ron Wolfson 7 x 9, 320 pp, Illus., Quality PB, 978-1-58023-164-0 **$19.99**

Hanukkah, 2nd Edition: The Family Guide to Spiritual Celebration
By Dr. Ron Wolfson   7 x 9, 240 pp, Illus., Quality PB, 978-1-58023-122-0 **$18.95**

The Jewish Family Fun Book, 2nd Edition
Holiday Projects, Everyday Activities, and Travel Ideas with Jewish Themes
By Danielle Dardashti and Roni Sarig; Illus. by Avi Katz
6 x 9, 304 pp, 70+ b/w illus. & diagrams, Quality PB, 978-1-58023-333-0 **$18.99**

Passover

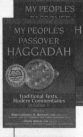

My People's Passover Haggadah
Traditional Texts, Modern Commentaries
Edited by Rabbi Lawrence A. Hoffman, PhD, and David Arnow, PhD
A diverse and exciting collection of commentaries on the traditional Passover Haggadah—in two volumes!
Vol. 1: 7 x 10, 304 pp, HC, 978-1-58023-354-5 **$24.99**
Vol. 2: 7 x 10, 320 pp, HC, 978-1-58023-346-0 **$24.99**

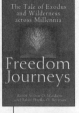

Freedom Journeys: The Tale of Exodus and Wilderness across Millennia
By Rabbi Arthur O. Waskow and Rabbi Phyllis O. Berman
Explores how the story of Exodus echoes in our own time, calling us to relearn and rethink the Passover story through social-justice, ecological, feminist and interfaith perspectives. 6 x 9, 288 pp, HC, 978-1-58023-445-0 **$24.99**

Leading the Passover Journey: The Seder's Meaning Revealed,
the Haggadah's Story Retold   By Rabbi Nathan Laufer
Uncovers the hidden meaning of the Seder's rituals and customs.
6 x 9, 224 pp, Quality PB, 978-1-58023-399-6 **$18.99**; HC, 978-1-58023-211-1 **$24.99**

Creating Lively Passover Seders, 2nd Edition: A Sourcebook of Engaging Tales,
Texts & Activities By David Arnow, PhD 7 x 9, 464 pp, Quality PB, 978-1-58023-444-3 **$24.99**

Passover, 2nd Edition: The Family Guide to Spiritual Celebration
By Dr. Ron Wolfson with Joel Lurie Grishaver 7 x 9, 416 pp, Quality PB, 978-1-58023-174-9 **$19.95**

The Women's Passover Companion: Women's Reflections on the Festival of Freedom
Edited by Rabbi Sharon Cohen Anisfeld, Tara Mohr and Catherine Spector; Foreword by Paula E. Hyman
6 x 9, 352 pp, Quality PB, 978-1-58023-231-9 **$19.99**; HC, 978-1-58023-128-2 **$24.95**

The Women's Seder Sourcebook: Rituals & Readings for Use at the Passover Seder
Edited by Rabbi Sharon Cohen Anisfeld, Tara Mohr and Catherine Spector
6 x 9, 384 pp, Quality PB, 978-1-58023-232-6 **$19.99**

Life Cycle
Marriage/Parenting/Family/Aging

The New Jewish Baby Album: Creating and Celebrating the Beginning of a Spiritual Life—A Jewish Lights Companion
By the Editors at Jewish Lights; Foreword by Anita Diamant; Preface by Rabbi Sandy Eisenberg Sasso
A spiritual keepsake that will be treasured for generations. More than just a memory book, *shows you how—and why it's important*—to create a Jewish home and a Jewish life. 8 x 10, 64 pp, Deluxe Padded HC, Full-color illus., 978-1-58023-138-1 **$19.95**

The Jewish Pregnancy Book: A Resource for the Soul, Body & Mind during Pregnancy, Birth & the First Three Months *By Sandy Falk, MD, and Rabbi Daniel Judson, with Steven A. Rapp* Medical information, prayers and rituals for each stage of pregnancy. 7 x 10, 208 pp, b/w photos, Quality PB, 978-1-58023-178-7 **$16.95**

Celebrating Your New Jewish Daughter: Creating Jewish Ways to Welcome Baby Girls into the Covenant—New and Traditional Ceremonies *By Debra Nussbaum Cohen; Foreword by Rabbi Sandy Eisenberg Sasso* 6 x 9, 272 pp, Quality PB, 978-1-58023-090-2 **$18.95**

The New Jewish Baby Book, 2nd Edition: Names, Ceremonies & Customs—A Guide for Today's Families *By Anita Diamant* 6 x 9, 320 pp, Quality PB, 978-1-58023-251-7 **$19.99**

Parenting as a Spiritual Journey: Deepening Ordinary and Extraordinary Events into Sacred Occasions *By Rabbi Nancy Fuchs-Kreimer, PhD*
6 x 9, 224 pp, Quality PB, 978-1-58023-016-2 **$17.99**

Parenting Jewish Teens: A Guide for the Perplexed
By Joanne Doades Explores the questions and issues that shape the world in which today's Jewish teenagers live and offers constructive advice to parents.
6 x 9, 176 pp, Quality PB, 978-1-58023-305-7 **$16.99**

Judaism for Two: A Spiritual Guide for Strengthening and Celebrating Your Loving Relationship *By Rabbi Nancy Fuchs-Kreimer, PhD, and Rabbi Nancy H. Wiener, DMin; Foreword by Rabbi Elliot N. Dorff, PhD*
Addresses the ways Jewish teachings can enhance and strengthen committed relationships. 6 x 9, 224 pp, Quality PB, 978-1-58023-254-8 **$16.99**

The Creative Jewish Wedding Book, 2nd Edition: A Hands-On Guide to New & Old Traditions, Ceremonies & Celebrations *By Gabrielle Kaplan-Mayer*
9 x 9, 288 pp, b/w photos, Quality PB, 978-1-58023-398-9 **$19.99**

Divorce Is a Mitzvah: A Practical Guide to Finding Wholeness and Holiness When Your Marriage Dies *By Rabbi Perry Netter; Afterword by Rabbi Laura Geller*
6 x 9, 224 pp, Quality PB, 978-1-58023-172-5 **$16.95**

Embracing the Covenant: Converts to Judaism Talk About Why & How
By Rabbi Allan Berkowitz and Patti Moskovitz 6 x 9, 192 pp, Quality PB, 978-1-879045-50-7 **$16.95**

The Guide to Jewish Interfaith Family Life: An InterfaithFamily.com Handbook
Edited by Ronnie Friedland and Edmund Case
6 x 9, 384 pp, Quality PB, 978-1-58023-153-4 **$18.95**

A Heart of Wisdom: Making the Jewish Journey from Midlife through the Elder Years
Edited by Susan Berrin; Foreword by Rabbi Harold Kushner
6 x 9, 384 pp, Quality PB, 978-1-58023-051-3 **$18.95**

Introducing My Faith and My Community: The Jewish Outreach Institute Guide for the Christian in a Jewish Interfaith Relationship
By Rabbi Kerry M. Olitzky 6 x 9, 176 pp, Quality PB, 978-1-58023-192-3 **$16.99**

Making a Successful Jewish Interfaith Marriage: The Jewish Outreach Institute Guide to Opportunities, Challenges and Resources *By Rabbi Kerry M. Olitzky with Joan Peterson Littman*
6 x 9, 176 pp, Quality PB, 978-1-58023-170-1 **$16.95**

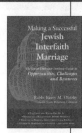

A Man's Responsibility: A Jewish Guide to Being a Son, a Partner in Marriage, a Father and a Community Leader *By Rabbi Joseph B. Meszler*
6 x 9, 192 pp, Quality PB, 978-1-58023-435-1 **$16.99**; HC, 978-1-58023-362-0 **$21.99**

So That Your Values Live On: Ethical Wills and How to Prepare Them
Edited by Rabbi Jack Riemer and Rabbi Nathaniel Stampfer
6 x 9, 272 pp, Quality PB, 978-1-879045-34-7 **$18.99**

Bible Stories / Folktales

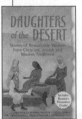

Abraham's Bind & Other Bible Tales of Trickery, Folly, Mercy and Love *by Michael J. Caduto*

New retellings of episodes in the lives of familiar biblical characters explore relevant life lessons. 6 x 9, 224 pp, HC, 978-1-59473-186-0 **$19.99**

Daughters of the Desert: Stories of Remarkable Women from Christian, Jewish and Muslim Traditions *by Claire Rudolf Murphy, Meghan Nuttall Sayres, Mary Cronk Farrell, Sarah Conover and Betsy Wharton*

Breathes new life into the old tales of our female ancestors in faith. Uses traditional scriptural passages as starting points, then with vivid detail fills in historical context and place. Chapters reveal the voices of Sarah, Hagar, Huldah, Esther, Salome, Mary Magdalene, Lydia, Khadija, Fatima and many more. Historical fiction ideal for readers of all ages.

5½ x 8½, 192 pp, Quality PB, 978-1-59473-106-8 **$14.99** Inc. reader's discussion guide
HC, 978-1-893361-72-0 **$19.95**

The Triumph of Eve & Other Subversive Bible Tales *by Matt Biers-Ariel*

These engaging retellings of familiar Bible stories are witty, often hilarious and always profound. They invite you to grapple with questions and issues that are often hidden in the original texts.

5½ x 8½, 192 pp, Quality PB, 978-1-59473-176-1 **$14.99**

Also available: **The Triumph of Eve Teacher's Guide**
8½ x 11, 44 pp, PB, 978-1-59473-152-5 **$8.99**

Wisdom in the Telling

Finding Inspiration and Grace in Traditional Folktales and Myths Retold
by Lorraine Hartin-Gelardi
6 x 9, 192 pp, HC, 978-1-59473-185-3 **$19.99**

Religious Etiquette / Reference

How to Be a Perfect Stranger, 5th Edition: The Essential Religious Etiquette Handbook *Edited by Stuart M. Matlins and Arthur J. Magida*

The indispensable guidebook to help the well-meaning guest when visiting other people's religious ceremonies. A straightforward guide to the rituals and celebrations of the major religions and denominations in the United States and Canada from the perspective of an interested guest of any other faith, based on information obtained from authorities of each religion. Belongs in every living room, library and office. Covers:

African American Methodist Churches • Assemblies of God • Bahá'í Faith • Baptist • Buddhist • Christian Church (Disciples of Christ) • Christian Science (Church of Christ, Scientist) • Churches of Christ • Episcopalian and Anglican • Hindu • Islam • Jehovah's Witnesses • Jewish • Lutheran • Mennonite/Amish • Methodist • Mormon (Church of Jesus Christ of Latter-day Saints) • Native American/First Nations • Orthodox Churches • Pentecostal Church of God • Presbyterian • Quaker (Religious Society of Friends) • Reformed Church in America/Canada • Roman Catholic • Seventh-day Adventist • Sikh • Unitarian Universalist • United Church of Canada • United Church of Christ

"The things Miss Manners forgot to tell us about religion."

—*Los Angeles Times*

"Finally, for those inclined to undertake their own spiritual journeys ... tells visitors what to expect."   —*New York Times*

6 x 9, 432 pp, Quality PB, 978-1-59473-294-2 **$19.99**

The Perfect Stranger's Guide to Funerals and Grieving Practices: A Guide to Etiquette in Other People's Religious Ceremonies *Edited by Stuart M. Matlins*
6 x 9, 240 pp, Quality PB, 978-1-893361-20-1 **$16.95**

The Perfect Stranger's Guide to Wedding Ceremonies: A Guide to Etiquette in Other People's Religious Ceremonies *Edited by Stuart M. Matlins*
6 x 9, 208 pp, Quality PB, 978-1-893361-19-5 **$16.95**

Meditation

Jewish Meditation Practices for Everyday Life
Awakening Your Heart, Connecting with God
By Rabbi Jeff Roth
Offers a fresh take on meditation that draws on life experience and living life with greater clarity as opposed to the traditional method of rigorous study.
6 x 9, 224 pp, Quality PB, 978-1-58023-397-2 **$18.99**

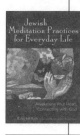

The Handbook of Jewish Meditation Practices
A Guide for Enriching the Sabbath and Other Days of Your Life
By Rabbi David A. Cooper Easy-to-learn meditation techniques.
6 x 9, 208 pp, Quality PB, 978-1-58023-102-2 **$16.95**

Discovering Jewish Meditation, 2nd Edition
Instruction & Guidance for Learning an Ancient Spiritual Practice
By Nan Fink Gefen, PhD 6 x 9, 208 pp, Quality PB, 978-1-58023-462-7 **$16.99**

Meditation from the Heart of Judaism
Today's Teachers Share Their Practices, Techniques, and Faith
Edited by Avram Davis 6 x 9, 256 pp, Quality PB, 978-1-58023-049-0 **$16.95**

Ritual/Sacred Practices

The Jewish Dream Book: The Key to Opening the Inner Meaning of Your Dreams *By Vanessa L. Ochs, PhD, with Elizabeth Ochs; Illus. by Kristina Swarner*
Instructions for how modern people can perform ancient Jewish dream practices and dream interpretations drawn from the Jewish wisdom tradition.
8 x 8, 128 pp, Full-color illus., Deluxe PB w/ flaps, 978-1-58023-132-9 **$16.95**

God in Your Body: Kabbalah, Mindfulness and Embodied Spiritual Practice
By Jay Michaelson
The first comprehensive treatment of the body in Jewish spiritual practice and an essential guide to the sacred.
6 x 9, 272 pp, Quality PB, 978-1-58023-304-0 **$18.99**

The Book of Jewish Sacred Practices: CLAL's Guide to Everyday & Holiday Rituals & Blessings *Edited by Rabbi Irwin Kula and Vanessa L. Ochs, PhD*
6 x 9, 368 pp, Quality PB, 978-1-58023-152-7 **$18.95**

Jewish Ritual: A Brief Introduction for Christians
By Rabbi Kerry M. Olitzky and Rabbi Daniel Judson
5½ x 8½, 144 pp, Quality PB, 978-1-58023-210-4 **$14.99**

The Rituals & Practices of a Jewish Life: A Handbook for Personal Spiritual Renewal *Edited by Rabbi Kerry M. Olitzky and Rabbi Daniel Judson*
6 x 9, 272 pp, Illus., Quality PB, 978-1-58023-169-5 **$18.95**

The Sacred Art of Lovingkindness: Preparing to Practice
By Rabbi Rami Shapiro 5½ x 8½, 176 pp, Quality PB, 978-1-59473-151-8 **$16.99**
(A book from SkyLight Paths, Jewish Lights' sister imprint)

Science Fiction/Mystery & Detective Fiction

Criminal Kabbalah: An Intriguing Anthology of Jewish Mystery & Detective Fiction *Edited by Lawrence W. Raphael; Foreword by Laurie R. King*
All-new stories from twelve of today's masters of mystery and detective fiction—sure to delight mystery buffs of all faith traditions.
6 x 9, 256 pp, Quality PB, 978-1-58023-109-1 **$16.95**

Mystery Midrash: An Anthology of Jewish Mystery & Detective Fiction
Edited by Lawrence W. Raphael; Preface by Joel Siegel
6 x 9, 304 pp, Quality PB, 978-1-58023-055-1 **$16.95**

Wandering Stars: An Anthology of Jewish Fantasy & Science Fiction
Edited by Jack Dann; Introduction by Isaac Asimov
6 x 9, 272 pp, Quality PB, 978-1-58023-005-6 **$18.99**

More Wandering Stars: An Anthology of Outstanding Stories of Jewish Fantasy and Science Fiction *Edited by Jack Dann; Introduction by Isaac Asimov*
6 x 9, 192 pp, Quality PB, 978-1-58023-063-6 **$16.95**

Spirituality/Prayer

Making Prayer Real: Leading Jewish Spiritual Voices on Why Prayer Is Difficult and What to Do about It By Rabbi Mike Comins
A new and different response to the challenges of Jewish prayer, with "best prayer practices" from Jewish spiritual leaders of all denominations.
6 x 9, 320 pp, Quality PB, 978-1-58023-417-7 **$18.99**

Witnesses to the One: The Spiritual History of the *Sh'ma*
By Rabbi Joseph B. Meszler; Foreword by Rabbi Elyse Goldstein
6 x 9, 176 pp, Quality PB, 978-1-58023-400-9 **$16.99**; HC, 978-1-58023-309-5 **$19.99**

My People's Prayer Book Series: Traditional Prayers, Modern Commentaries *Edited by Rabbi Lawrence A. Hoffman, PhD*
Provides diverse and exciting commentary to the traditional liturgy. Will help you find new wisdom in Jewish prayer, and bring liturgy into your life. Each book includes Hebrew text, modern translations and commentaries from all perspectives of the Jewish world.

Vol. 1—The *Sh'ma* and Its Blessings
7 x 10, 168 pp, HC, 978-1-879045-79-8 **$29.99**
Vol. 2—The *Amidah* 7 x 10, 240 pp, HC, 978-1-879045-80-4 **$24.95**
Vol. 3—*P'sukei D'zimrah* (Morning Psalms)
7 x 10, 240 pp, HC, 978-1-879045-81-1 **$29.99**
Vol. 4—*Seder K'riat Hatorah* (The Torah Service)
7 x 10, 264 pp, HC, 978-1-879045-82-8 **$29.99**
Vol. 5—*Birkhot Hashachar* (Morning Blessings)
7 x 10, 240 pp, HC, 978-1-879045-83-5 **$24.95**
Vol. 6—*Tachanun* and Concluding Prayers
7 x 10, 240 pp, HC, 978-1-879045-84-2 **$24.95**
Vol. 7—Shabbat at Home 7 x 10, 240 pp, HC, 978-1-879045-85-9 **$24.95**
Vol. 8—*Kabbalat Shabbat* (Welcoming Shabbat in the Synagogue)
7 x 10, 240 pp, HC, 978-1-58023-121-3 **$24.99**
Vol. 9—Welcoming the Night: *Minchah* and *Ma'ariv* (Afternoon and Evening Prayer) 7 x 10, 272 pp, HC, 978-1-58023-262-3 **$24.99**
Vol. 10—Shabbat Morning: *Shacharit* and *Musaf* (Morning and Additional Services) 7 x 10, 240 pp, HC, 978-1-58023-240-1 **$29.99**

Spirituality/Lawrence Kushner

I'm God; You're Not: Observations on Organized Religion & Other Disguises of the Ego
6 x 9, 256 pp, HC, 978-1-58023-441-2 **$21.99**

The Book of Letters: A Mystical Hebrew Alphabet
Popular HC Edition, 6 x 9, 80 pp, 2-color text, 978-1-879045-00-2 **$24.95**
Collector's Limited Edition, 9 x 12, 80 pp, gold-foil-embossed pages, w/ limited-edition silkscreened print, 978-1-879045-04-0 **$349.00**

The Book of Miracles: A Young Person's Guide to Jewish Spiritual Awareness
6 x 9, 96 pp, 2-color illus., HC, 978-1-879045-78-1 **$16.95** *For ages 9–13*

The Book of Words: Talking Spiritual Life, Living Spiritual Talk
6 x 9, 160 pp, Quality PB, 978-1-58023-020-9 **$18.99**

Eyes Remade for Wonder: A Lawrence Kushner Reader *Introduction by Thomas Moore*
6 x 9, 240 pp, Quality PB, 978-1-58023-042-1 **$18.95**

God Was in This Place & I, i Did Not Know: Finding Self, Spirituality and Ultimate Meaning 6 x 9, 192 pp, Quality PB, 978-1-879045-33-0 **$16.95**

Honey from the Rock: An Introduction to Jewish Mysticism
6 x 9, 176 pp, Quality PB, 978-1-58023-073-5 **$16.95**

Invisible Lines of Connection: Sacred Stories of the Ordinary
5½ x 8½, 160 pp, Quality PB, 978-1-879045-98-9 **$15.95**

Jewish Spirituality: A Brief Introduction for Christians
5½ x 8½, 112 pp, Quality PB, 978-1-58023-150-3 **$12.95**

The River of Light: Jewish Mystical Awareness
6 x 9, 192 pp, Quality PB, 978-1-58023-096-4 **$16.95**

The Way Into Jewish Mystical Tradition
6 x 9, 224 pp, Quality PB, 978-1-58023-200-5 **$18.99**; HC, 978-1-58023-029-2 **$21.95**

Spirituality

Repentance: The Meaning and Practice of *Teshuvah*
By Dr. Louis E. Newman; Foreword by Rabbi Harold M. Schulweis; Preface by Rabbi Karyn D. Kedar
Examines both the practical and philosophical dimensions of *teshuvah*, Judaism's core religious-moral teaching on repentance, and its value for us—Jews and non-Jews alike—today. 6 x 9, 256 pp, HC, 978-1-58023-426-9 **$24.99**

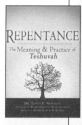

Tanya, the Masterpiece of Hasidic Wisdom
Selections Annotated & Explained
Translation & Annotation by Rabbi Rami Shapiro; Foreword by Rabbi Zalman M. Schachter-Shalomi
Brings the genius of *Tanya,* one of the most powerful books of Jewish wisdom, to anyone seeking to deepen their understanding of the soul.
5½ x 8½, 240 pp, Quality PB, 978-1-59473-275-1 **$16.99**
(A book from SkyLight Paths, Jewish Lights' sister imprint)

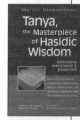

Aleph-Bet Yoga: Embodying the Hebrew Letters for Physical and Spiritual Well-Being
By Steven A. Rapp; Foreword by Tamar Frankiel, PhD, and Judy Greenfeld; Preface by Hart Lazer
7 x 10, 128 pp, b/w photos, Quality PB, Lay-flat binding, 978-1-58023-162-6 **$16.95**

A Book of Life: Embracing Judaism as a Spiritual Practice
By Rabbi Michael Strassfeld 6 x 9, 544 pp, Quality PB, 978-1-58023-247-0 **$19.99**

Bringing the Psalms to Life: How to Understand and Use the Book of Psalms
By Rabbi Daniel F. Polish, PhD 6 x 9, 208 pp, Quality PB, 978-1-58023-157-2 **$16.95**

Does the Soul Survive? A Jewish Journey to Belief in Afterlife, Past Lives & Living with Purpose *By Rabbi Elie Kaplan Spitz; Foreword by Brian L. Weiss, MD*
6 x 9, 288 pp, Quality PB, 978-1-58023-165-7 **$16.99**

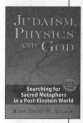

First Steps to a New Jewish Spirit: Reb Zalman's Guide to Recapturing the Intimacy & Ecstasy in Your Relationship with God *By Rabbi Zalman M. Schachter-Shalomi with Donald Gropman* 6 x 9, 144 pp, Quality PB, 978-1-58023-182-4 **$16.95**

Foundations of Sephardic Spirituality: The Inner Life of Jews of the Ottoman Empire
By Rabbi Marc D. Angel, PhD 6 x 9, 224 pp, Quality PB, 978-1-58023-341-5 **$18.99**

God & the Big Bang: Discovering Harmony between Science & Spirituality
By Dr. Daniel C. Matt 6 x 9, 216 pp, Quality PB, 978-1-879045-89-7 **$16.99**

God in Our Relationships: Spirituality between People from the Teachings of Martin Buber *By Rabbi Dennis S. Ross* 5½ x 8½, 160 pp, Quality PB, 978-1-58023-147-3 **$16.95**

The Jewish Lights Spirituality Handbook: A Guide to Understanding, Exploring & Living a Spiritual Life *Edited by Stuart M. Matlins*
What exactly is "Jewish" about spirituality? How do I make it a part of my life? Fifty of today's foremost spiritual leaders share their ideas and experience with us.
6 x 9, 456 pp, Quality PB, 978-1-58023-093-3 **$19.99**

Judaism, Physics and God: Searching for Sacred Metaphors in a Post-Einstein World
By Rabbi David W. Nelson 6 x 9, 352 pp, Quality PB, inc. reader's discussion guide,
978-1-58023-306-4 **$18.99**; HC, 352 pp, 978-1-58023-252-4 **$24.99**

Meaning & Mitzvah: Daily Practices for Reclaiming Judaism through Prayer, God, Torah, Hebrew, Mitzvot and Peoplehood *By Rabbi Goldie Milgram*
7 x 9, 336 pp, Quality PB, 978-1-58023-256-2 **$19.99**

Minding the Temple of the Soul: Balancing Body, Mind, and Spirit through Traditional Jewish Prayer, Movement, and Meditation *By Tamar Frankiel, PhD, and Judy Greenfeld*
7 x 10, 184 pp, Illus., Quality PB, 978-1-879045-64-4 **$18.99**

One God Clapping: The Spiritual Path of a Zen Rabbi *By Rabbi Alan Lew with Sherril Jaffe*
5½ x 8½, 336 pp, Quality PB, 978-1-58023-115-2 **$16.95**

The Soul of the Story: Meetings with Remarkable People
By Rabbi David Zeller 6 x 9, 288 pp, HC, 978-1-58023-272-2 **$21.99**

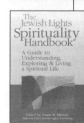

There Is No Messiah ... and You're It: The Stunning Transformation of Judaism's Most Provocative Idea *By Rabbi Robert N. Levine, DD*
6 x 9, 192 pp, Quality PB, 978-1-58023-255-5 **$16.99**

These Are the Words: A Vocabulary of Jewish Spiritual Life
By Rabbi Arthur Green, PhD 6 x 9, 304 pp, Quality PB, 978-1-58023-107-7 **$18.95**

Theology/Philosophy

The God Who Hates Lies: Confronting & Rethinking Jewish Tradition
By Dr. David Hartman with Charlie Buckholtz
The world's leading Modern Orthodox Jewish theologian probes the deepest questions at the heart of what it means to be a human being and a Jew.
6 x 9, 208 pp, HC, 978-1-58023-455-9 **$24.99**

Jewish Theology in Our Time: A New Generation Explores the Foundations and Future of Jewish Belief *Edited by Rabbi Elliot J. Cosgrove, PhD; Foreword by Rabbi David J. Wolpe; Preface by Rabbi Carole B. Balin, PhD*
A powerful and challenging examination of what Jews can believe—by a new generation's most dynamic and innovative thinkers.
6 x 9, 240 pp, HC, 978-1-58023-413-9 **$24.99**

Maimonides—Essential Teachings on Jewish Faith & Ethics: The Book of Knowledge & the Thirteen Principles of Faith—Annotated & Explained
Translation and Annotation by Rabbi Marc D. Angel, PhD Opens up for us Maimonides's views on the nature of God, providence, prophecy, free will, human nature, repentance and more. 5½ x 8½, 224 pp, Quality PB Original, 978-1-59473-311-6 **$18.99**

The Death of Death: Resurrection and Immortality in Jewish Thought
By Rabbi Neil Gillman, PhD 6 x 9, 336 pp, Quality PB, 978-1-58023-081-0 **$18.95**

Doing Jewish Theology: God, Torah & Israel in Modern Judaism *By Rabbi Neil Gillman, PhD*
6 x 9, 304 pp, Quality PB, 978-1-58023-439-9 **$18.99**

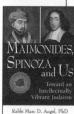

Hasidic Tales: Annotated & Explained *Translation & Annotation by Rabbi Rami Shapiro*
5½ x 8¼, 240 pp, Quality PB, 978-1-893361-86-7 **$16.95***

A Heart of Many Rooms: Celebrating the Many Voices within Judaism
By Dr. David Hartman 6 x 9, 352 pp, Quality PB, 978-1-58023-156-5 **$19.95**

The Hebrew Prophets: Selections Annotated & Explained
Translation & Annotation by Rabbi Rami Shapiro; Foreword by Rabbi Zalman M. Schachter-Shalomi
5½ x 8¼, 224 pp, Quality PB, 978-1-59473-037-5 **$16.99***

Maimonides, Spinoza and Us: Toward an Intellectually Vibrant Judaism
By Rabbi Marc D. Angel, PhD A challenging look at two great Jewish philosophers and what their thinking means to our understanding of God, truth, revelation and reason. 6 x 9, 224 pp, HC, 978-1-58023-411-5 **$24.99**

A Living Covenant: The Innovative Spirit in Traditional Judaism
By Dr. David Hartman 6 x 9, 368 pp, Quality PB, 978-1-58023-011-7 **$25.00**

Love and Terror in the God Encounter: The Theological Legacy of Rabbi Joseph B. Soloveitchik *By Dr. David Hartman* 6 x 9, 240 pp, Quality PB, 978-1-58023-176-3 **$19.95**

A Touch of the Sacred: A Theologian's Informal Guide to Jewish Belief
By Dr. Eugene B. Borowitz and Frances W. Schwartz
6 x 9, 256 pp, Quality PB, 978-1-58023-416-0 **$16.99**; HC, 978-1-58023-337-8 **$21.99**

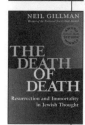

Traces of God: Seeing God in Torah, History and Everyday Life *By Rabbi Neil Gillman, PhD*
6 x 9, 240 pp, Quality PB, 978-1-58023-369-9 **$16.99**

Your Word Is Fire: The Hasidic Masters on Contemplative Prayer
Edited and translated by Rabbi Arthur Green, PhD, and Barry W. Holtz
6 x 9, 160 pp, Quality PB, 978-1-879045-25-5 **$15.95**

I Am Jewish
Personal Reflections Inspired by the Last Words of Daniel Pearl
Almost 150 Jews—both famous and not—from all walks of life, from all around the world, write about many aspects of their Judaism.
Edited by Judea and Ruth Pearl 6 x 9, 304 pp, Deluxe PB w/ flaps, 978-1-58023-259-3 **$18.99**
Download a free copy of the *I Am Jewish Teacher's Guide* at www.jewishlights.com.

Hannah Senesh: Her Life and Diary, The First Complete Edition
By Hannah Senesh; Foreword by Marge Piercy; Preface by Eitan Senesh; Afterword by Roberta Grossman
6 x 9, 368 pp, b/w photos, Quality PB, 978-1-58023-342-2 **$19.99**

***A book from SkyLight Paths, Jewish Lights' sister imprint*

Inspiration

God of Me: Imagining God throughout Your Lifetime
By Rabbi David Lyon Helps you cut through preconceived ideas of God and dogmas that stifle your creativity when thinking about your personal relationship with God. 6 x 9, 176 pp, Quality PB, 978-1-58023-452-8 **$16.99**

The God Upgrade: Finding Your 21st-Century Spirituality in Judaism's 5,000-Year-Old Tradition *By Rabbi Jamie Korngold; Foreword by Rabbi Harold M. Schulweis* A provocative look at how our changing God concepts have shaped every aspect of Judaism. 6 x 9, 176 pp, Quality PB, 978-1-58023-443-6 **$15.99**

The Seven Questions You're Asked in Heaven: Reviewing and Renewing Your Life on Earth *By Dr. Ron Wolfson* An intriguing and entertaining resource for living a life that matters. 6 x 9, 176 pp, Quality PB, 978-1-58023-407-8 **$16.99**

Happiness and the Human Spirit: The Spirituality of Becoming the Best You Can Be *By Rabbi Abraham J. Twerski, MD* Shows you that true happiness is attainable once you stop looking outside yourself for the source. 6 x 9, 176 pp, Quality PB, 978-1-58023-404-7 **$16.99**; HC, 978-1-58023-343-9 **$19.99**

A Formula for Proper Living: Practical Lessons from Life and Torah *By Rabbi Abraham J. Twerski, MD* 6 x 9, 144 pp, HC, 978-1-58023-402-3 **$19.99**

The Bridge to Forgiveness: Stories and Prayers for Finding God and Restoring Wholeness *By Rabbi Karyn D. Kedar* 6 x 9, 176 pp, Quality PB, 978-1-58023-451-1 **$16.99**

The Empty Chair: Finding Hope and Joy—Timeless Wisdom from a Hasidic Master, Rebbe Nachman of Breslov *Adapted by Moshe Mykoff and the Breslov Research Institute* 4 x 6, 128 pp, Deluxe PB w/ flaps, 978-1-879045-67-5 **$9.99**

The Gentle Weapon: Prayers for Everyday and Not-So-Everyday Moments— Timeless Wisdom from the Teachings of the Hasidic Master, Rebbe Nachman of Breslov *Adapted by Moshe Mykoff and S. C. Mizrahi, together with the Breslov Research Institute* 4 x 6, 144 pp, Deluxe PB w/ flaps, 978-1-58023-022-3 **$9.99**

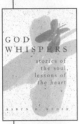

God Whispers: Stories of the Soul, Lessons of the Heart *By Rabbi Karyn D. Kedar* 6 x 9, 176 pp, Quality PB, 978-1-58023-088-9 **$15.95**

God's To-Do List: 103 Ways to Be an Angel and Do God's Work on Earth *By Dr. Ron Wolfson* 6 x 9, 144 pp, Quality PB, 978-1-58023-301-9 **$16.99**

Jewish Stories from Heaven and Earth: Inspiring Tales to Nourish the Heart and Soul *Edited by Rabbi Dov Peretz Elkins* 6 x 9, 304 pp, Quality PB, 978-1-58023-363-7 **$16.99**

Life's Daily Blessings: Inspiring Reflections on Gratitude and Joy for Every Day, Based on Jewish Wisdom *By Rabbi Kerry M. Olitzky* $4\frac{1}{2}$ x $6\frac{1}{2}$, 368 pp, Quality PB, 978-1-58023-396-5 **$16.99**

Restful Reflections: Nighttime Inspiration to Calm the Soul, Based on Jewish Wisdom *By Rabbi Kerry M. Olitzky and Rabbi Lori Forman-Jacobi* $4\frac{1}{2}$ x $6\frac{1}{2}$, 448 pp, Quality PB, 978-1-58023-091-9 **$15.95**

Sacred Intentions: Morning Inspiration to Strengthen the Spirit, Based on Jewish Wisdom *By Rabbi Kerry M. Olitzky and Rabbi Lori Forman-Jacobi* $4\frac{1}{2}$ x $6\frac{1}{2}$, 448 pp, Quality PB, 978-1-58023-061-2 **$16.99**

Kabbalah/Mysticism

Jewish Mysticism and the Spiritual Life: Classical Texts, Contemporary Reflections *Edited by Dr. Lawrence Fine, Dr. Eitan Fishbane and Rabbi Or N. Rose* Inspirational and thought-provoking materials for contemplation, discussion and action. 6 x 9, 256 pp, HC, 978-1-58023-434-4 **$24.99**

Ehyeh: A Kabbalah for Tomorrow *By Rabbi Arthur Green, PhD* 6 x 9, 224 pp, Quality PB, 978-1-58023-213-5 **$18.99**

The Gift of Kabbalah: Discovering the Secrets of Heaven, Renewing Your Life on Earth *By Tamar Frankiel, PhD* 6 x 9, 256 pp, Quality PB, 978-1-58023-141-1 **$16.95**

Seek My Face: A Jewish Mystical Theology *By Rabbi Arthur Green, PhD* 6 x 9, 304 pp, Quality PB, 978-1-58023-130-5 **$19.95**

Zohar: Annotated & Explained *Translation & Annotation by Dr. Daniel C. Matt; Foreword by Andrew Harvey* $5\frac{1}{2}$ x $8\frac{1}{2}$, 176 pp, Quality PB, 978-1-893361-51-5 **$15.99**
(A book from SkyLight Paths, Jewish Lights' sister imprint)

See also *The Way Into Jewish Mystical Tradition* in The Way Into... Series.

Judaism / Christianity / Interfaith

Christians & Jews—Faith to Faith: Tragic History, Promising Present, Fragile Future *By Rabbi James Rudin*
A probing examination of Christian-Jewish relations that looks at the major issues facing both faith communities. 6 x 9, 288 pp, HC, 978-1-58023-432-0 **$24.99**

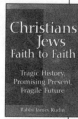

Religion Gone Astray: What We Found at the Heart of Interfaith
By Pastor Don Mackenzie, Rabbi Ted Falcon and Imam Jamal Rahman
Probes more deeply into the problem aspects of our religious institutions—specifically exclusivity, violence, inequality of men and women, and homophobia—to provide a profound understanding of the nature of what divides us.
6 x 9, 192 pp, Quality PB, 978-1-59473-317-8 **$16.99***

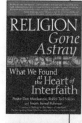

Getting to the Heart of Interfaith: The Eye-Opening, Hope-Filled Friendship of a Pastor, a Rabbi and an Imam
By Rabbi Ted Falcon, Pastor Don Mackenzie and Imam Jamal Rahman
Presents ways we can work together to transcend the differences that have divided us historically. 6 x 9, 192 pp, Quality PB, 978-1-59473-263-8 **$16.99***

How to Do Good & Avoid Evil: A Global Ethic from the Sources of Judaism
By Hans Küng and Rabbi Walter Homolka 6 x 9, 224 pp, HC, 978-1-59473-255-3 **$19.99***

Claiming Earth as Common Ground: The Ecological Crisis through the Lens of Faith *By Rabbi Andrea Cohen-Kiener* 6 x 9, 192 pp, Quality PB, 978-1-59473-261-4 **$16.99***

Modern Jews Engage the New Testament: Enhancing Jewish Well-Being in a Christian Environment *By Rabbi Michael J. Cook, PhD* 6 x 9, 416 pp, HC, 978-1-58023-313-2 **$29.99**

The Changing Christian World: A Brief Introduction for Jews
By Rabbi Leonard A. Schoolman 5½ x 8½, 176 pp, Quality PB, 978-1-58023-344-6 **$16.99**

Christians & Jews in Dialogue: Learning in the Presence of the Other
By Mary C. Boys and Sara S. Lee
6 x 9, 240 pp, Quality PB, 978-1-59473-254-6 **$18.99**; HC, 978-1-59473-144-0 **21.99***

Disaster Spiritual Care: Practical Clergy Responses to Community, Regional and National Tragedy *Edited by Rabbi Stephen B. Roberts, BCJC, and Rev. Willard W. C. Ashley Sr., DMin, DH*
6 x 9, 384 pp, HC, 978-1-59473-240-9 **$40.00***

How to Be a Perfect Stranger, 5th Edition: The Essential Religious Etiquette Handbook *Edited by Stuart M. Matlins and Arthur J. Magida*
6 x 9, 432 pp, Quality PB, 978-1-59473-294-2 **$19.99***

InterActive Faith: The Essential Interreligious Community-Building Handbook
Edited by Rev. Bud Heckman with Rori Picker Neiss
6 x 9, 304 pp, Quality PB, 978-1-59473-273-7 **$16.99**; HC, 978-1-59473-237-9 **$29.99***

Introducing My Faith and My Community
The Jewish Outreach Institute Guide for the Christian in a Jewish Interfaith Relationship
By Rabbi Kerry M. Olitzky 6 x 9, 176 pp, Quality PB, 978-1-58023-192-3 **$16.99**

The Jewish Approach to Repairing the World (*Tikkun Olam*)
A Brief Introduction for Christians *By Rabbi Elliot N. Dorff, PhD, with Rev. Cory Willson*
5½ x 8½, 256 pp, Quality PB, 978-1-58023-349-1 **$16.99**

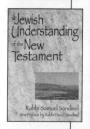

The Jewish Connection to Israel, the Promised Land: A Brief Introduction for Christians *By Rabbi Eugene Korn, PhD* 5½ x 8½, 192 pp, Quality PB, 978-1-58023-318-7 **$14.99**

Jewish Holidays: A Brief Introduction for Christians *By Rabbi Kerry M. Olitzky and Rabbi Daniel Judson* 5½ x 8½, 176 pp, Quality PB, 978-1-58023-302-6 **$16.99**

Jewish Ritual: A Brief Introduction for Christians *By Rabbi Kerry M. Olitzky and Rabbi Daniel Judson* 5½ x 8½, 144 pp, Quality PB, 978-1-58023-210-4 **$14.99**

A Jewish Understanding of the New Testament *By Rabbi Samuel Sandmel; Preface by Rabbi David Sandmel* 5½ x 8½, 368 pp, Quality PB, 978-1-59473-048-1 **$19.99***

Righteous Gentiles in the Hebrew Bible: Ancient Role Models for Sacred Relationships *By Rabbi Jeffrey K. Salkin; Foreword by Rabbi Harold M. Schulweis; Preface by Phyllis Tickle* 6 x 9, 192 pp, Quality PB, 978-1-58023-364-4 **$18.99**

We Jews and Jesus: Exploring Theological Differences for Mutual Understanding
By Rabbi Samuel Sandmel; Preface by Rabbi David Sandmel
6 x 9, 192 pp, Quality PB, 978-1-59473-208-9 **$16.99**

*A book from SkyLight Paths, Jewish Lights' sister imprint

JEWISH LIGHTS BOOKS ARE AVAILABLE FROM BETTER BOOKSTORES. TRY YOUR BOOKSTORE FIRST.

About Jewish Lights

People of all faiths and backgrounds yearn for books that attract, engage, educate, and spiritually inspire.

Our principal goal is to stimulate thought and help all people learn about who the Jewish People are, where they come from, and what the future can be made to hold. While people of our diverse Jewish heritage are the primary audience, our books speak to people in the Christian world as well and will broaden their understanding of Judaism and the roots of their own faith.

We bring to you authors who are at the forefront of spiritual thought and experience. While each has something different to say, they all say it in a voice that you can hear.

Our books are designed to welcome you and then to engage, stimulate, and inspire. We judge our success not only by whether or not our books are beautiful and commercially successful, but by whether or not they make a difference in your life.

For your information and convenience, at the back of this book we have provided a list of other Jewish Lights books you might find interesting and useful. They cover all the categories of your life:

Bar/Bat Mitzvah
Bible Study / Midrash
Children's Books
Congregation Resources
Current Events / History
Ecology / Environment
Fiction: Mystery, Science Fiction
Grief / Healing
Holidays / Holy Days
Inspiration
Kabbalah / Mysticism / Enneagram

Life Cycle
Meditation
Men's Interest
Parenting
Prayer / Ritual / Sacred Practice
Social Justice
Spirituality
Theology / Philosophy
Travel
Twelve Steps
Women's Interest

Stuart M. Matlins, Publisher

Or phone, fax, mail or e-mail to: **JEWISH LIGHTS Publishing**
Sunset Farm Offices, Route 4 • P.O. Box 237 • Woodstock, Vermont 05091
Tel: (802) 457-4000 • Fax: (802) 457-4004 • www.jewishlights.com
Credit card orders: (800) 962-4544 (8:30AM–5:30PM EST Monday–Friday)
Generous discounts on quantity orders. SATISFACTION GUARANTEED. Prices subject to change.

For more information about each book, visit our website at www.jewishlights.com